Diving & Snorkeling
Turks & Caicos

Steve Rosenberg

D1367133

LONELY PLANET PUBLICATIONS
Melbourne • Oakland • London • Paris

Diving & Snorkeling Turks & Caicos
- A Lonely Planet Pisces Book

2nd Edition – October 2001
1st Edition – 1993 Gulf Publishing Company

Published by
Lonely Planet Publications
90 Maribyrnong St., Footscray, Victoria 3011, Australia

Other offices
150 Linden Street, Oakland, California 94607, USA
10a Spring Place, London NW5 3BH, UK
1 rue du Dahomey, 75011 Paris, France

Photographs
by Steve Rosenberg unless otherwise noted

Front cover photograph
Diver with bluestriped grunts at The Library, Grand Turk,
by Steve Rosenberg

Back cover photographs
Loggerhead turtle, by Steve Rosenberg
Diver and barrel sponge at The Gully, West Caicos,
    by Steve Rosenberg
Tiki huts along the Providenciales shore,
    by Piers van der Walt

The images in this guide are available for licensing
    from Lonely Planet Images
email: lpi@lonelyplanet.com.au

ISBN 1 86450 294 0

text & maps © Lonely Planet 2001
photographs © photographers as indicated 2001
dive site maps are Transverse Mercator projection

LONELY PLANET and the Lonely Planet logo are
trademarks of Lonely Planet Publications Pty Ltd.

Printed by H&Y Printing Ltd., Hong Kong

Contents

Diving Health & Safety   32

Diving in the Turks & Caicos   35

Providenciales Dive Sites   42

West Caicos Dive Sites   54

Author

Steve Rosenberg

SHANNON ROSENBERG

Steve has been a professional underwater photographer and photojournalist since 1980, when he began writing articles on travel, photography and nature for various U.S. publications. He is a member of the Society of American Travel Writers and has published several books and hundreds of articles. He has also won more than 250 awards for his photography in international competitions. Thousands of his images have appeared in books, magazines and posters, as well as stamps and artwork worldwide. He lives in Northern California and has explored the underwater world around the globe for more than 30 years. Steve also practices law in Alameda, California, and has been actively involved in diver access litigation in California.

From the Author

I'd like to thank my many friends, dive buddies and family members for their support, encouragement and never-ending patience throughout the course of this project. In particular I would like to thank my darling wife, Darlene, my daughter, Shannon, and my stepdaughter, Jessica, for their assistance with research, modeling, diving, companionship and hugs; and my good friends Piers and Annette van der Walt for their unending assistance and support. I would also like to thank the Aggressor Fleet, Peter Hughes and Terri Huber of Peter Hughes Diving, Philip Shearer of Big Blue, Michele Taylor with the Ministry of Natural Resources, Cecil Ingrahm and Connie Rus of Sea Eye Diving, Everette Freitas and Dale Barker of Oasis Divers, Art Pickering of Provo Turtle Divers, and Turks Head Inn for their tremendous support and assistance. Finally I would like to thank my buddies Roslyn Bullas, Sarah Hubbard and David Lauterborn of Lonely Planet Publications, who have been very professional throughout and wonderful to work with.

Photography Notes

Steve's preferred photographic equipment includes Nikonos RS-AF cameras and lenses, Nikon SB-104 and Sea & Sea Strobes, with Ultralite arms and accessories. Most of the images in this book were shot on Fujichrome Velvia film for close-ups and Fujichrome Provia, Fujichrome Astia and Kodak Ektachrome E100SW for wide-angle photographs.

From the Publisher

This second edition was published in Lonely Planet's U.S. office under the guidance of Roslyn Bullas, the Pisces Books publishing manager. Sarah Hubbard edited the text and photos with buddy checks from David Lauterborn and Kevin Anglin. Emily Douglas designed the cover and the book's interior. Navigating the nautical charts was cartographer Brad Lodge with assistance from Rachel Driver and Sara Nelson. The Turks and Caicos Department of Environmental and Coastal Resources confirmed park boundary information. U.S. cartography manager Alex Guilbert supervised map production. Lindsay Brown reviewed the Marine Life section for scientific accuracy. Portions of the text were adapted from Lonely Planet's *Bahamas, Turks & Caicos*.

Pisces Pre-Dive Safety Guidelines

Before embarking on a scuba diving, skin diving or snorkeling trip, carefully consider the following to help ensure a safe and enjoyable experience:

- Possess a current diving certification card from a recognized scuba diving instructional agency (if scuba diving)
- Be sure you are healthy and feel comfortable diving
- Obtain reliable information about physical and environmental conditions at the dive site (e.g., from a reputable local dive operation)
- Be aware of local laws, regulations and etiquette about marine life and environment
- Dive at sites within your experience level; if possible, engage the services of a competent, professionally trained dive instructor or divemaster

Underwater conditions vary significantly from one region, or even site, to another. Seasonal changes can significantly alter site and dive conditions. These differences influence the way divers dress for a dive and what diving techniques they use.

There are special requirements for diving in any area, regardless of location. Before your dive, ask about environmental characteristics that can affect your diving and how trained local divers deal with these considerations.

Warning & Request

Things change—dive site conditions, regulations, topside information. Nothing stays the same for long. Your feedback on this book will be used to help update and improve the next edition. Excerpts from your correspondence may appear in *Planet Talk*, our quarterly newsletter, or *Comet*, our monthly email newsletter. Please let us know if you do not want your letter published or your name acknowledged.

Correspondence can be addressed to:
Lonely Planet Publications
Pisces Books
150 Linden Street
Oakland, CA 94607
email: pisces@lonelyplanet.com

Introduction

It was not so long ago that the Turks and Caicos Islands were a little-known destination. For many years the islands' tourist slogan was "Where on earth are the Turks and Caicos?" In a relatively short span of time these islands have gained a reputation as a top Caribbean diving destination—arguably one of the world's best.

With a dramatic increase in the number of weekly flights destined here, the proximity of the islands to several major U.S. gateway cities and the promise of an upgrade in the islands' airports, it is inevitable that the Turks and Caicos will experience a tourism boom. Hotels sprinkled throughout the islands provide about 2,500 rooms, but the Turks and Caicos Islands tourist board would like to double that number. While resort development is proceeding at a rapid pace on the main island of Providenciales (known locally as Provo), the other islands retain a sleepy, bucolic mood.

If you're not an investment banker or a drug smuggler, chances are you've come to the Turks and Caicos to dive the vertical walls or swim with sharks, dolphins and

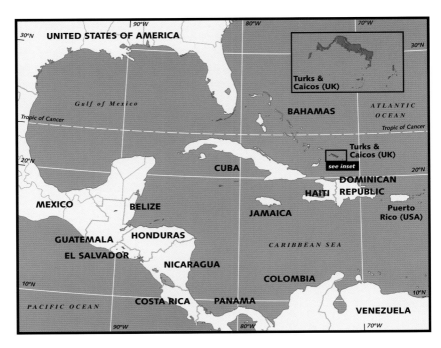

whales. You won't find many places in the Caribbean like it—where the diving is just as good as it was "way back when." Divers will discover sheer vertical walls, lots of big animals, and lush reefs with a spectacular array of colorful sponges and awesome corals, as well as myriad strange and unusual creatures.

Ashore, the Turks and Caicos are not the prettiest of the Caribbean islands, being mostly rocky, semi-barren and covered with cacti and thorny acacia trees. However, some areas possess incredible beauty. In 1999, *Condé Naste Traveller* rated the Turks and Caicos as having the best beaches in the world. The 200 miles (320km) of powdered-sugar sand beaches terrace gently into turquoise and emerald-green shallows, which change abruptly to deep blues where the ocean floor falls off into the depths. These islands are also a bird-watcher's and whale watcher's paradise. For fishing and dining, the waters offer wahoo, dolphin-fish (mahimahi), sailfish and kingfish. These are only a few of the many game species that cruise the shallow banks and deep water within a half-mile (1km) of shore. The bonefishing is superb and largely untapped.

Though just a fraction of the islands' possible dive sites, the 44 sites covered in this book represent many of the popular and interesting sites throughout the developed dive regions, including Providenciales, the west wall off of West Caicos, French Cay, South Caicos, Grand Turk and Salt Cay. Information about location, depth range, access and necessary skill level is provided for each site. The detailed dive site descriptions include information about each site's marine life and topography, special features, conditions and photo opportunities. The Marine Life sections offer a photo gallery of some of the Turks and Caicos' more common fish and invertebrates, as well as descriptions of a few hazardous species to watch out for. The Overview and Practicalities sections offer some useful background information, while the Activities & Attractions section suggests things to do when you are not diving.

The Turks and Caicos Islands' conch farm produces more than a million conchs a year.

Overview

PIERS VAN DER WALT

The Turks and Caicos, currently a British crown colony, are geographically part of the Bahama Banks, southeast of The Bahamas and separated from them by the deep, 30-mile-wide (50km-wide) Caicos Passage. The chain consists of eight islands and more than 40 small cays (pronounced both "kays" and "keys"), of which only eight are inhabited. Of the approximately 26,000 residents, 18,000 reside on Providenciales. Though it's just an 80- to 90-minute flight from Miami (closer than either Puerto Rico or the U.S. Virgin Islands), this once-obscure outpost has only recently begun to appear on tourist maps and divers' itineraries.

Geography

The Turks and Caicos consist of two island groups, the Turks Islands and the Caicos Islands, formed atop two separate limestone pinnacles, or banks, each surrounded by broken strips of coral reef. The banks are separated by the Turks Island Passage (also known as the Columbus Passage), a deepwater channel 22 miles (35km) wide and 7,000ft (2,100m) deep. The land mass of the islands totals 193 sq miles (500 sq km), only 10% of the total area the banks cover.

To the west is the Caicos island group, perched atop the Caicos Bank, comprising an arc of islands and cays including (west to east) West Caicos, Providenciales, North Caicos, Middle Caicos, East Caicos and South Caicos. These islands are separated from one another by shallow waterways. Four of these islands (Providenciales, North Caicos, Middle Caicos and South Caicos) and two cays (Pine Cay and Parrot Cay) are inhabited.

Sitting atop the Turks Bank to the east of the Turks Island Passage is the Turks island group, comprising several small islands and cays. The two largest, Grand Turk and tiny Salt Cay, are inhabited.

Geology

The islands and cays of the Turks and Caicos are merely above-water portions of a series of broad submerged plateaus, or banks. Deep ocean waters surround each shallow bank. Unlike the neighboring mountainous and geologically active islands to the southeast, the Turks and Caicos were created by the slow growth of organic reef communities.

11

Reef Terminology

Though it can sometimes seem like a foreign language, comprehending reef terminology will help you understand some of the Turks and Caicos' most common underwater geologic features.

Most of the islands and cays in the Turks and Caicos lie along the outside edges of the expansive underwater plateaus known as the Caicos Bank and the Turks Bank. These banks are rather shallow, typically between 20 and 30ft (6 and 9m) deep. The *hardpan*, the porous limestone material that makes up most of the banks, is visible in the shallows around most of the islands and cays. It has little if any covering of sand. Above the waterline, many of the islands are fringed by a weathered, jagged *ironshore*. Ironshore is a formation of consolidated coral, mollusk shells and limestone.

Deepwater passages and open ocean that plummet to depths between 5,000 and 7,000ft (1,500 to 2,100m) border the outer edges of the banks. Most of the dive sites in the Turks and Caicos are wall dives along these *drop-offs* on the leeward side of the cays and islands.

Moorings are placed or drilled into the *back reef*, a relatively stable area between the shore and the drop-off. The back reef is often flat or gently sloping. Some back reefs have well-defined *spur-and-groove formations*—parallel coral ridges with sand or rubble channels running between them. Other back reefs consist of a sand-and-rubble bottom punctuated with scattered coral heads and stands of pillar or soft corals. Occasionally the back reef is simply a vast sandy bottom with garden eels and other sand creatures.

Typically, seaward of the back reef is a *fringing* (or *fringe*) *reef*, which grows fairly close to shore along the edge, or lip, of the drop-off. Fringing reefs can vary greatly in width and height. The fringe reef usually refers to the coral ridge on top of the lip of the drop-off. The *buttress* is the part of the coral buildup on the fore slope or front of the wall.

A few sites, such as Providenciales' Grace Bay, are along a *barrier reef*, which rises to the surface or even breaks the surface at low tide. The landward side of the barrier reef usually makes for a great, protected snorkeling area. Seaward of the barrier reef, the sea floor falls off steeply to the *mixed zone*, or *buttress zone*. In Grace Bay this buttress zone is formed by massive spur-and-groove coral formations. Beyond the buttress zone, the *fore reef* lies between 30 and 100ft (10 to 30m), sometimes deeper.

Tiki huts left from a French game show sit atop the eroding limestone ironshore.

All of the islands and cays in the Turks and Caicos are composed entirely of limestone, created by millions of years of coral growth. Seawater contains high concentrations of calcium carbonate, one of the most common rock-forming minerals on earth. Wherever oceans are warm, well lit, oxygenated and nutrient rich, marine organisms thrive and utilize the readily available minerals to synthesize protective outer casings, or exoskeletons, as a defense against predators. Over countless generations, these calcium deposits have built up into layer upon layer of carbonic rock known as limestone. The reef structure is covered with a thin veneer of living corals that continue the reef-growing process.

The process of reef building and limestone deposition has occurred in the Turks and Caicos since the early Cretaceous period, approximately 130 million years ago. Boreholes drilled into the limestone have penetrated 20,000ft (7,000m) of continuous reef sequence overlying a volcanic foundation, suggesting that the first reef growth in the Turks and Caicos may have occurred as a fringing reef around an ancient volcano, similar to the atolls in the Pacific. As the volcano slowly submerged, the sustained tropical environment allowed the reef growth to proliferate.

Ecology

Cacti punctuate much of the islands' landscape.

The Turks and Caicos are predominantly semiarid, notably Salt Cay and much of South Caicos and Grand Turk, which were denuded of vegetation to dissuade rainfall during the heyday of the salt industry. The remaining vegetation is tenacious and well adapted to the dry conditions—cacti thrive. The larger, middle islands of North, Middle and East Caicos are more lush. Native vegetation varies from island to island, according to variations in rainfall. Much of the islands, notably the southern halves of North, Middle and East Caicos, are composed of creeks, sand flats, lagoons and marshy wetlands. Most of the sandy beaches—some of the finest on the planet—are on shores facing the open ocean.

The vast wetlands in the southern portions of the Caicos Islands are ideal feeding grounds for shorebirds, and the numerous uninhabited cays throughout the chain make perfect nesting sites for seabirds. Of the more than 175 bird species seen here, 78 are migratory land birds. Ospreys, pelicans and frigate birds are common in the islands. Flamingos are also common on North Caicos and South Caicos.

The largest of the native animals are the rock iguanas, which eke out a living on many of the uninhabited islands. You'll see almost as many donkeys, wild horses and cattle as humans, although they stay in the wilds. Their forebears once carried 25lb (11kg) burlap bags of salt from the ponds to the warehouses and docks. Having earned their rest, they were set free.

History

The Turks and Caicos' earliest residents were the Lucayans (from the native *lukku-cairi*, or "island people"), descendants of the South American Arawak Indians. These peaceful people had migrated to the Caribbean and then north to The Bahamas and the Turks and Caicos Islands around the 6th or 7th centuries to escape the attacks of the warlike Caribs, from whom the region gets its name. The Lucayans lived primarily off the sea, and evolved skills as potters, carvers, weavers and boat builders.

Locals claim that the islands were Christopher Columbus' first landfall in 1492. Some argue for Grand Turk, where a monument attempts to cast the claim in stone. Experts, however, have debunked the theory. Persuasive arguments based upon Columbus' written descriptions of "the island," the vegetation and the inhabitants, as well as studies of prevailing currents and wind patterns, suggest that Columbus may have crossed the Turks Island Passage (also known as the Columbus Passage), viewing the Caicos Islands and coming ashore near Northwest Point on Providenciales, before moving on to The Bahamas.

An old cannon is testament to the islands' checkered past.

In any event, the docile Lucayans soon fell prey to the slave trade and European diseases, against which they had no defense. By the early 1500s the entire native population had either died or been physically removed.

The island group was a pawn in the power struggles between the French, Spaniards and British. For several centuries ownership bounced like a ping-pong ball, landing finally with Great Britain. But lying windward of the main sailing routes, possessing no gold or decent anchorages and lacking sufficient rain for growing sugar, the islands were viewed as unimportant specks. They remained virtually uninhabited until 1678, when a group of Bermudians settled and began to extract salt and timber. Salt traders cleared the land and created the *salinas* (salt-drying pans) that still exist on several islands. Most of the salt went aboard swift sloops to supply the cod-fishing industries of New England and Canada's Maritime Provinces.

In 1710 the Spaniards captured the islands, then sailed away. The Bermudians returned and prospered. Like their northerly neighbors, the islands became a base for notorious pirates, who were not averse to sacking the wealthy salt merchants' homes. The pirates' depredations invoked a French attack in 1753, and France claimed the islands. Though repelled the following year by a British warship from the Carolinas, the French briefly occupied Grand Turk again in 1778 and 1783.

Following the American Revolution, the Bermudians were joined by a wave of colonial loyalists. They brought their slaves, established cotton plantations throughout the islands and built the King's Road, which ran across North Caicos to the end of East Caicos. But the plantation era was short-lived. By 1820 the cotton crop had failed. The majority of planters moved on. Many left their slaves behind, and eventually they too became salt rakers. About the middle of the 19th century a whaling industry flourished, with its base in the Ambergris Cays, southwest of South Caicos.

The islands became a formal part of The Bahamas in 1799, but in 1848, following a petition by Turks and Caicos residents, they became self-governing under the supervision of the governor of Jamaica. In 1872 Jamaica annexed the islands.

The islands remained tied to Jamaica until well into the 20th century. The U.S. military built airstrips during WWII, bringing brief prosperity to the islands. The islands slumbered in obscurity until 1962, when astronaut John Glenn splashed down just off Grand Turk, putting the islands in the international spotlight. That same year the islands again became linked to The Bahamas.

About the same time (1966), the islands were "discovered" by seven millionaires (including Teddy Roosevelt III and a couple of Du Ponts), who leased land from the British government, built a small airstrip for their private planes and constructed a deep-water anchorage for their yachts and those of friends escaping the rigors of East Coast winters. When those friends arrived in larger numbers than their hosts could accommodate, the intimate Third Turtle Inn was built to relieve the pressure. By the 1970s Provo was the near-private domain of a group of wealthy escape artists from long-john climates.

In 1973 the Turks and Caicos became a crown colony of Great Britain. Meanwhile, Count Ferdinand Czernin, son of the last prime minister of the Austro-Hungarian Empire, ferreted out a tiny dot on the map—Pine Cay, northeast of Provo—on which he planned a Walden Pond-like resort. After his death, it became the exclusive Meridian Club, a prizewinning resort still frequented by the sophisticated elite.

In 1984 Club Med opened its doors on Providenciales, and the Turks and Caicos started to boom. In the blink of an eye the islands, which had lacked electricity, acquired satellite TV. Today bulldozers and half-poured foundations line the roads of Provo, the center of the tourism boom. Tourism is and will probably continue to be the islands' number one industry. Fortunately, the Turks and Caicos government realized that the region's greatest asset is the environment itself. The government is dedicated to balancing development with environmental sensitivity.

Where Did the Name "Turks & Caicos" Come From?

Some people claim that piracy accounts for the islands' name: "Turks" for the name of a group of Mediterranean pirates and "Caicos" for the name of their boats.

It is more likely that "Turks" refers to the species of native cactus whose scarlet blossom resembles the red flat-topped hat, or fez, worn by men in Turkey. The Turk's head cactus (shown below), with its nearly cylindrical red blossom, grew abundantly on the islands at the time the Spaniards first arrived.

"Caicos" is said to come from a mispronunciation of the Spanish word for "little islands," *cayos*.

PIERS VAN DER WALT

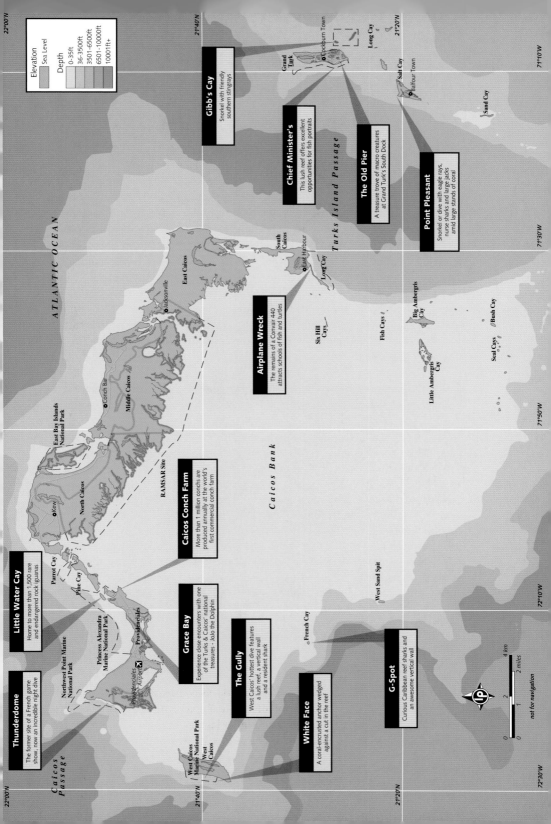

Practicalities

Climate

The Turks and Caicos Islands enjoy year-round sunshine with prevailing easterly breezes courtesy of the Atlantic trade winds. The seasons are usually pretty dry and warm. The islands average between 20 and 40 inches (50 and 100cm) of rain per year, most of which falls in the summer months. The average humidity is about 35%. The hottest months are July through October, when the trade winds are at their lightest. Water temperatures tend to parallel the air temperatures, with the warmest waters from July through September. This is also the hurricane season. Official announcements of hurricanes are broadcast on Turks and Caicos radio (on Grand Turk 94.9 FM and on Providenciales 105.9 FM).

Typical Weather Patterns for the Turks & Caicos Islands

January to late March or early April: Air temperature during this time of the year normally ranges between 75°F and 80°F (24 and 27°C). However, the temperature may dip if a strong northern cold front moves in. Water temperatures are between 75°F and 78°F (24 and 26°C). A cold front out of the north will also make the ocean more choppy.

Middle or late April to June: Air temperatures are usually 82 to 84°F (28 to 29°C) during the day. The water temperature climbs to an average of 80°F (27°C).

July to September: This is usually the hurricane season. Air temperatures continue to climb, ranging from 82°F to 87°F (28 to 31°C). Water temperatures are also at their year-round warmest, between 84°F and 86°F (29 and 30°C).

October to December: Air temperatures are usually between 72°F and 85°F (22 and 29°C). Water temperatures are usually between 78 and 82°F (26 and 28°C).

Language

English is the official language of the Turks and Caicos Islands. However, quite a few of the locals speak a combination of Creole, French and Spanish. There are also a number of discernable accents and other languages spoken by expatriates who have relocated to these islands, as well as by tourists who come from all over the world.

Getting There

There are four international airports in the Turks and Caicos Islands. The main airport is on the island of Providenciales, with more than 40 flights arriving each week. Grand Turk, South Caicos and North Caicos also have airports with smaller runways. Delta Airlines and American Airlines are the major international carriers. Bahamas Air offers weekly trips between Provo and Miami. Lynx Air currently connects Fort Lauderdale with both Provo and Grand Turk.

Regularly scheduled service and charter flights provide frequent connections between the islands. Turks and Caicos Air, SkyKing and InterIsland Airways not only fly between islands, but also have regularly scheduled flights to other Caribbean islands. Travel to the Turks and Caicos is also possible through The Bahamas, Cuba, Haiti and the Dominican Republic.

For divers, especially those traveling with photographic and video gear, luggage is sometimes a concern. The larger airlines allow several checked items per person, but occasionally charge per bag if you have more than two per person. You are normally allowed to take two small carry-on bags, but this is discouraged if the planes are full. If you are flying on the smaller airlines, you will be required to pay for each piece of luggage, and carry-ons are generally not permitted. Check with the carrier when making reservations to determine if there are restrictions and how much additional baggage costs.

Small planes provide transportation between the islands.

Gateway City – Providenciales

The majority of visitors to the Turks and Caicos arrive in Provo, the main island. Many never get beyond its shores, and it is easy to see why. The island boasts a score of resorts along one of the world's most incredible beaches. Away from the beaches, Provo is rather nondescript, with low rugged hills and ridges, carpeted with prickly pear cacti and scrub unfolding down to the sea.

The island is shaped like a wedge, narrowing to the northeast. The north shore is a gentle, concave curve lined with white-sand beaches. The southern shore is largely composed of sounds and lakes. The western half of Provo is mostly barren wilderness, dramatic and well worth exploring, with one national park and a national reserve. Provo's best wall diving is along this west coast within the Northwest Point Marine National Park.

The main town, sprawling, soulless namesake Providenciales, sits in the middle of the island. It's a modern town with a haphazard layout. Pockets of makeshift shacks are interspersed among more upscale homes. Turtle Cove, about a mile northeast of downtown, is a node for tourist services and has Provo's premier marina. Several of Provo's dive services are based here.

The resort scene grips the north shore of 5-mile-long Grace Bay, with its blindingly white sand and unbelievably turquoise waters. The bay begins east of

Turtle Cove is a hub for tourist services and has Provo's premier marina.

Providenciales

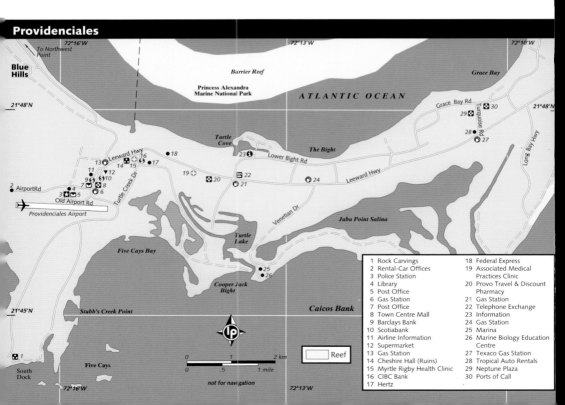

1	Rock Carvings	18	Federal Express
2	Rental-Car Offices	19	Associated Medical
3	Police Station		Practices Clinic
4	Library	20	Provo Travel & Discount
5	Post Office		Pharmacy
6	Gas Station	21	Gas Station
7	Post Office	22	Telephone Exchange
8	Town Centre Mall	23	Information
9	Barclays Bank	24	Gas Station
10	Scotiabank	25	Marina
11	Airline Information	26	Marine Biology Education
12	Supermarket		Centre
13	Gas Station	27	Texaco Gas Station
14	Cheshire Hall (Ruins)	28	Tropical Auto Rentals
15	Myrtle Rigby Health Clinic	29	Neptune Plaza
16	CIBC Bank	30	Ports of Call
17	Hertz		

Turtle Cove and is lined with an unbroken, snow-white beach backed by well-spaced hotels. You'll find several dive sites and excellent snorkeling areas near Grace Bay's barrier reef.

Getting Around

Getting around on the islands is easy. Taxis are available throughout the islands, but you need to be mindful of the high fares. To avoid any confusion, settle on the fare to your destination before you get in the taxi. Drivers will be happy to provide a guided tour. On the island of Providenciales you can also get around by *jitney*, the local equivalent to a bus. These air-conditioned mini-vans have standard routes and are much more economical than taxis.

Rental cars, motorcycles, scooters and bicycles are available on Provo and Grand Turk. A government tax is levied on all vehicle rentals, and insurance is mandatory. You can legally drive here if you have a valid driver's license from your country of residence.

Driving in the Turks and Caicos is relatively easy. There are no traffic signals and only a few stop signs. Compared to most countries' speed limits, the maximum speeds here are slow—40mph (64km/h) on highways, and 20mph (32km/h) on residential streets and in downtown areas. Visitors should keep in mind that, though the cars' steering wheels are on the left side, driving is done on the left-hand side of the road here. If you are used to driving on the right, this can be quite confusing when negotiating one of the traffic circles or making a right-hand turn. In the evening many of the streets are minimally lit, and drivers opt to use their high beams. Many of the roads are unpaved, so if you are considering exploring beaches and parks in the remote parts of the islands, you should probably rent a four-wheel-drive vehicle.

Entry

A passport and valid return ticket are generally required for entry. However, visitors from North America may enter without a passport if they provide their birth certificate and one piece of photo identification. The customs and immigration employees in the Turks and Caicos are generally very agreeable, making entry smooth and hassle-free.

A departure tax of US$15 per person is charged for everyone over the age of 12, payable in cash only. To avoid hassles when you leave, it is advisable to put this amount into your passport at the start of your trip.

Time

The Turks and Caicos Islands are on Eastern Standard Time (EST), five hours behind Greenwich Mean Time (GMT), and observe daylight saving time. When it is noon in the Turks and Caicos, it is 9am in San Francisco, noon in New York, 5pm in London and 4am the next day in Sydney.

Money

U.S. dollars are the official currency used in the islands, along with the Turks and Caicos crown and quarter (coins issued by the treasury), all of which are legal tender. There are no restrictions on the amount of money that visitors can bring into the country. Foreign currency is easily changed at most banks. Most credit cards are widely accepted, especially on Provo and Grand Turk, as are traveler's checks. Elsewhere you may need to operate on a cash-only basis. It is advisable to carry some cash, as not all types of vendors will accept credit cards or traveler's checks—taxi fares, admission fees to various attractions or stopping for a bite to eat are much more easily paid for with cash.

Taxes & Tipping

There is a 9% hotel tax and a customary 10% gratuity (tip) associated with most lodging and restaurants. This will usually be automatically added to your hotel or restaurant bill. Larger restaurants and those connected with hotels will invariably add a 19% gratuity to your bill. When paying, look to see if the tip has already been included in the total charges.

Electricity

The electrical current is 110 volts/60 cycles, as it is in the United States and Canada. Most outlets accept ungrounded plugs with two parallel blades (one slightly larger than the other). Most hotel electrical outlets have the third grounding hole to accommodate electrical chargers, computers and small appliances. However, it is a good idea to pack any adapters or converters that you might require.

Weights & Measures

Although the Turks and Caicos are a British crown colony, for the most part they use imperial measurements rather than the metric system. Gas is measured in gallons, and distances and speeds are posted in miles. Temperature is typically measured in Fahrenheit, length in feet and yards, and weight in pounds and ounces. Please refer to the conversion chart on the inside back cover for metric equivalents.

Dive shops and live-aboards measure distances in nautical miles, weights in pounds, air pressure in pounds per square inch (PSI) and depths in feet. Divers accustomed to the metric system should expect to perform their own conversions.

In this book both imperial and metric measurements are given, except for specific references in dive site descriptions, which are given in imperial units only.

What to Bring

General Supplies

Days are usually warm, bright and sunny year-round in the Turks and Caicos. However, evenings can get cooler, especially in the winter months (December through early March), so bring a windbreaker, shell or sweatshirt. When it comes to island fashion, the rule of thumb is very casual. Swimsuits, shorts and light, comfortable tops are what you will typically wear. Most of your time will be spent outdoors—diving, snorkeling, exploring or just kicking back. If you plan on hiking, bring hardy rubber-soled shoes or sneakers. Sturdy dive booties are good to have not only for diving, but also for kayak trips and eco-tours that may entail walking on a variety of abrasive, sharp or slippery surfaces.

Women might want to pack a light cotton dress and men a pair of lightweight slacks if you think you will go to one of the luxury resorts for dining or evening cocktails. However, none of the islands' hotel restaurants require jackets or ties.

Though vacation necessities such as sunscreen and film are easy to find on Provo, they aren't always available on the other islands. It is always a good idea to pack required medications, a good decongestant, a hat, insect repellent, a small flashlight (for walking around at night), sunscreen and plenty of film and batteries.

Dive-Related Equipment

Many divers prefer to bring their own equipment to the Turks and Caicos, as top-notch rental scuba gear (such as dive computers and BCs) isn't always readily available. Dive computers are particularly handy here, since many of the dives can be deep—if you don't own a dive computer, rent one at home and bring it along. Also bring your own mask, fins and snorkel. Bringing your own equipment will ensure a proper fit, and you will enjoy diving more if you are comfortable with how the equipment works and know it has been maintained. That said, if you do need to rent gear, you'll find the best selection on Provo.

A 3mm full wetsuit is good for the cooler winter months (when the water temperature drops to the mid-70s Fahrenheit, or about 25°C), as well as for

---

Rough Fileclam Delivers

The Turks and Caicos pride themselves on the beauty of their incredible selection of collectable stamps. They have sponsored in-country international underwater photography competitions, and featured the winning entries in series of commemorative stamps. Photographers from all over the globe came to the Turks and Caicos Islands in 1997 and 1998 to participate in the  contest. The author's winning image of a rough fileclam is a colorful addition to the postal service's underwater series.

night dives or multiple consecutive dives. Even when the water temperature climbs into the low 80s (about 28°C), it is still nice to have a full wetsuit or dive skin for protection against things that sting, scrape or cut. Some divers even prefer the warmth of a drysuit, especially when diving four or more dives per day.

Underwater Photography

The Turks and Caicos are a favorite Caribbean dive destination for underwater photography. The conditions are excellent (calm water, decent visibility, lack of surge, etc.) and you'll find an exceptional variety of subjects to shoot.

The selection of macrophotography subjects rivals the much heralded "macro capitals of the world." Divers will not only find a laundry list of the usual suspects (e.g., tube worms, fire worms, flamingo tongues, hermit crabs, rough fileclams, Pederson shrimp, banded coral shrimp and arrow crabs), but also more unusual and fascinating subjects, such as seahorses, neck crabs, pygmy octopuses, nudibranchs, fingerprint cyphomas, shortnose batfish and frogfish.

Good visibility and calm water make the Turks and Caicos ideal for underwater photography.

Close-up photography is just as rewarding. The fish are plentiful and friendly. Many varieties of fish that are difficult to approach in other areas of the Caribbean, such as queen angelfish, queen triggerfish, scrawled filefish and whitespotted filefish, are at least cooperative if not overly friendly. The walls and fringing reefs offer tapestries of colors and shapes for both scenic and close-focus wide-angle photographs. You'll find great opportunities to photograph sharks, turtles, rays, barracuda, jacks and schooling fish in many areas of the islands.

All serious photographers know that it's a good idea to bring your own equipment and plenty of backup equipment, as well as plenty of film, extra batteries and spare parts. It's always better to bring too much rather than not have what you need. It's a good idea to assemble each system before you pack it, but even that doesn't guarantee that you won't need something else while on your trip.

Fortunately, several camera stores on Providenciales sell batteries and professional quality slide and print film, but film prices are steep. Fish Frames (☎ 649-946-4059), in Neptune Plaza near the Comfort Suites,

Providenciales, is the only operation that offers photography classes, rental equipment, repairs and maintenance and even digital scanning. A few of the dive operators on Provo and Grand Turk have some camera gear for rent. The *Turks and Caicos Aggressor* and the Peter Hughes live-aboards have a full range of photographic gear available. See the Listings section or check with the individual operators for details.

Business Hours

Government offices are generally open weekdays from 8am to 12:30pm and again from 2 to 4pm. Private offices and businesses are usually open from 8:30am to 5pm Monday through Saturday. Banks are open from 8:30am to 2:30pm Monday through Thursday, and from 8:30am to 12:30pm and 2:30 to 4:30pm Friday.

Accommodations

Lodging in the Turks and Caicos Islands ranges from quaint inns to high-end resorts. The variety is greatest on Provo, where you can choose among modern boutique hotels, intimate guesthouses, condominiums, Club Med and other all-inclusive resorts, as well as modest hotels. A 9% hotel tax plus 1% surcharge apply to all room rates. Most hotels add their own surcharge (usually about 20%) during the December/January holiday season. Many hotels also add a 10 to 20% service charge, also assessed on anything charged to your room.

Dining & Food

The Turks and Caicos offer an excellent variety of international cuisines. Of course, the bounty of the waters surrounding the islands dictates that fresh seafood is a prominent part of the most popular meals. Conch (pronounced "konk") dishes are a favorite with locals and visitors alike. You can enjoy this tasty shellfish prepared many ways, including conch salad, conch fritters, cracked conch, conch chowder and steamed conch. Wahoo and mahimahi are also among the most popular seafood dishes and are almost always available fresh from the day's catch.

Providenciales, the most populous island, has a number of excellent restaurants to choose from. Pub on the Bay (Smokey's), in the Blue Hills area, features native dishes and great seafood and is popular with the locals. Other favorites are Hemingway's, which is right on the beach at the Sands resort on Grace Bay, and The Terrace, which is in Turtle Cove at the Turtle Cove Inn.

Drinking water on most of the islands comes from rainwater collected off rooftops and kept in cisterns. Providenciales pipes purified water to homes and businesses. Also, most of the larger hotels have reverse osmosis equipment to make drinking water from salt water. Though tap water should be fine for brushing your teeth, it is a good idea to drink only bottled water, which is readily available in hotels and stores.

Boogaloo's Conch Shack

A fun, informative and tasty Provo outing is to head out along Blue Hills Road toward the Wheeland area and make a stop at Boogaloo's Conch Shack. Row upon row of upturned, glistening pink conch shells surround this open-air establishment.

Live conchs are kept in an ocean crawl, or underwater pen, just off the beach. You can don mask and snorkel to select your own or pick from the beachside stack of fresh conchs ready to be cleaned.

You can watch how the animal is removed from the shell and cleaned. A hole in the back of the shell is made with a pointed hammer. A knife is then used to release the animal's grip on the inside of the shell. The animal is pulled out of the shell by tugging on the muscular foot. The conch is then diced and marinated in lime juice and mixed with sliced onions, tomatoes, sweet peppers and other special ingredients to concoct an incredibly fresh and tasty conch salad. This preparation method has been used for more than 100 years.

Boogaloo also serves up conch fritters and a few other delicacies on demand. The operation sells up to 500 conchs weekly and has served visiting dignitaries, celebrities, divers and even traveling journalists.

Stop in for a snack at Boogaloo's Conch Shack.

Shopping

Although the Turks and Caicos are touted for their lack of commercial tourism, the discerning shopper can still find unique gifts and souvenirs. The myriad duty-free stores, boutiques and gift shops throughout Providenciales and to a lesser extent on Grand Turk contain countless great gifts. Most resorts and hotels have gift shops, boutiques and other stores within their complexes. On Providenciales, Ports of Call on Grace Bay Road and Central Square on the Leeward Highway offer a number of interesting boutiques and stores.

Quite a few stores carry a variety of handcrafted gifts, children's items, locally made crafts, jewelry and artwork. However, you have to look a lot harder for these here than in most tourist destinations. The handcrafted plait-and-sew style of straw weaving does survive, and handmade rag rugs and baskets are a great buy. The art scene is lively on Provo, where you can pick up some interesting and colorful Haitian paintings.

Activities & Attractions

Divers and nondivers alike will find many things to do and see in the Turks and Caicos Islands. Most activities and attractions are outdoors, giving visitors the opportunity to take advantage of the fabulous climate. Providenciales offers a greater choice of activities than the other islands. Most organized watersports (parasailing, kayaking, etc.) are on Provo. You can go on a few excellent nature excursions on North Caicos, Middle Caicos and South Caicos. The other islands offer little more than hiking, diving and snorkeling.

National Museum

If you visit Grand Turk, the Turks and Caicos National Museum (☎ 649-946-2160) at Front Street and Murphy Alley is well worth checking out. The museum is on the waterfront in the restored Guinep House, one of the oldest native stone buildings in the islands. The museum's exhibits include artifacts excavated from the Molasses Reef wreck, the oldest shipwreck in the Americas, discovered in 1982 on Molasses Reef on the edge of the Caicos Bank.

A visit to the museum is a great way to learn about the culture and history of the Turks and Caicos Islands. In addition to intriguing displays of artifacts from the days of Columbus to the Space Age, the museum also has areas for archaeological and historical research, artifact conservation and a shop offering a selection of books, maps, postcards and authentic island handicrafts. The museum is open weekdays from 10am to 4pm, and on Saturday from 10am to 1pm.

Caicos Conch Farm

Providenciales boasts the world's first conch farm (☎ 649-946-5330) found at the east end of the Leeward Highway. The Caicos Bank region once supplied 4 million conchs per year, but like elsewhere in the Caribbean, the supply has been overfished and harvests are declining. Most divers who have visited the Caribbean over the last 10 to 20 years have noticed a serious depletion in the number of conchs seen in shallow sandy areas. The conch farm was developed in 1984 to alleviate pressure on the natural population. Since 1990 the farm has produced "100% farm-raised conchs" for export to Florida markets and also for consumption within the Turks and Caicos. More recently it has started to export to new markets, including China and Japan.

Conch-farm technology has developed steadily for more than 15 years. Today the farm produces 1 million queen conchs a year and maintains an inventory of about 3 million on site. The farm's 16 employees operate the egg farm, the hatchery facility, post-larvae grow-out buildings, onshore nursery ponds, a sub-sea maturation pasture and a fresh-product processing facility.

Egg masses, which contain up to 500,000 eggs each, are harvested from the egg farm by divers and then transported to the hatchery. In the wild, only one conch out of each egg mass survives to adulthood. The rest are eaten by a long list of predators including lobsters, stingrays, crabs, octopuses, turtles and porcupinefish.

The Queen Conch

The queen conch, *Strobus gigas*, is a beautiful, pink-lipped shellfish that inhabits shallow sandy bottoms in the clean saltwater that surrounds The Bahamas, Bermuda, Florida and the Turks and Caicos Islands, and throughout the Caribbean. You can generally find them on seagrass beds and sand flats between 3 and 100ft (1 and 30m).

The exterior of this shellfish is orangish, although it sometimes appears sand colored because of algal growth and an accumulation of silt and debris on the outer shell. The opening in the shell is a glistening rosy pink color. The animal propels itself along the bottom with a single muscular foot. It has two very curious eyes, which appear at the tips of stalks. The average size of queen conchs is between 7 and 9 inches (18 to 23cm) long, but they sometimes grow to 12 inches (30cm).

Conch is described as having a rather delicate seafood flavor, similar in texture and taste to abalone—sweet and a little fishy. It's one of the most protein-rich, low-fat foods available. It's believed that the conch was an important food source in the Caribbean long before Christopher Columbus came to the New World. The queen conch has become uncommon in some areas because of overfishing.

A curious queen conch peeks its eyestalks from its pink-lipped shell.

In the hatchery, 6 million free-swimming baby conchs (in their larval stage) are produced annually. During the next phase of production, which takes place in the post-larval facilities, free-swimming larvae are induced to change to bottom-dwelling baby conchs. At any given time this metamorphosis facility is capable of maturing 1 million juvenile conchs from ⅙ to ¾ inch (4mm to 2cm) in length. The post-larvae survival rate is more than 80%. The 36 onshore nursery ponds are capable of holding 1.5 million juvenile conchs, which grow from ¾ to 3¼ inches (2 to 8cm) over a 12-month period. At this point the conchs are placed in the sub-sea pasture, a 60-acre (24-hectare) fenced pen just offshore, where they are protected from most predators. The conchs grow here until they are ready for export, usually within a year or two.

Cheshire Hall Plantation

In the 1790s British loyal-ists established the Cheshire Hall Plantation to farm cotton on Providenciales. By 1820 most of the planters moved from the islands, having found that the thin soil, insects and hurricanes devastated their efforts to bring in a viable crop. You can visit the plantation's ruins, which are in downtown Provo on the south side of Leeward Highway's west end, next to the Myrtle Rigby Health Clinic.

Cheshire Hall Plantation makes for an interesting outing.

Eco-Adventures

Eco-adventures are the perfect way to experience the outdoors firsthand while learning about local flora, fauna and marine life from the experts. Excursions can include boating, hiking, biking, snorkeling and kayaking, or a combination of these. Some popular guided trips leave from Leeward Marina on Provo: kayak tours through the mangrove channels; visits to the rock iguana sanctuary on Little Water Cay in the Princess Alexandra Marine National Park; kayak trips to the conch farm; a land tour and snorkeling around the mangrove cays and in the shallows of the northern barrier reef; and biking and hiking tours in the reserves and caves on Middle Caicos.

Big Blue Unlimited (bigblue@tciway.tcin, ☎ 649-946-5034), in the Leeward Marina, works with REEF (Reef Environmental Education Foundation), offering reef fish identification courses in association with PADI's Project AWARE.

Whale Watching

The Turks and Caicos Islands are one of the few places in the world where humans are allowed to interact with humpbacks in their natural environment. Every year from January through March, humpback whales migrate from northern polar waters to the Silver Banks and the Mouchoir Banks (southeast of the Turks and Caicos) where they breed and give birth. The whales' migratory path brings them through the deep passages on either side of the Turks Bank. During their migration, whales frequently make appearances at dive sites in the Turks and Caicos. The live-aboard dive boats *Turks and Caicos Aggressor* and the *Wind Dancer* (operated by Peter Hughes) offer special trips to the Silver Banks, where you can snorkel with these majestic animals.

PIERS VAN DER WALT

Humpback whales pass the Turks and Caicos during their migration.

Little Water Cay

Little Water Cay, at the northeast end of Provo, is a nature reserve within the borders of the Princess Alexandra Marine National Park. The 150-acre cay has two small interior lakes surrounded by native trees and plants. It is home to more than 1,500 of a rare type of rock iguana found only in the Turks and Caicos Islands. Their burrows and nesting chambers are underground. A raised board-walk trail allows visitors to take a close look at these reptiles without trampling their homes. Visitors can also get a bird's-eye view of osprey nests and the surrounding island from raised viewing towers. Little Water Cay is easily accessible from the Leeward Marina—contact Big Blue Unlimited for kayak or boat excursions to Little Water Cay.

The Rock Iguanas

Rock iguanas once inhabited much of the Turk and Caicos Islands. The colonies on larger islands were wiped out by development, which destroyed their natural habitats, and by newly introduced predators, such as domestic cats and dogs. These now-endangered rock iguanas are found on uninhabited cays and islands only.

The Turks and Caicos National Trust sponsors a "Little Water Cay Initiative" to raise US$50,000 annually for preservation of the rock iguana *Cyclura carnata*, the endangered endemic iguana species found only on Little Water Cay. The iguanas living there have become a major tourist lure for the 150-acre cay. Fort George Cay (near Little Water Cay) and the Ambergris Cays (south of South Caicos) also are protected iguana reserves.

The rock iguana is the largest native land animal in the Turks and Caicos Islands. Approximately 50,000 common rock iguanas—the Caribbean's largest and healthiest remaining population—still live in the Turks and Caicos. They are believed to have a life span of about 15 years and begin breeding at the age of 6 or 7. These animals are harmless vegetarians that feed on berries, leaves and fruit. They leave their shallow underground burrows to sun themselves and to feed. Though generally shy, on Little Water Cay they are used to humans and will allow you to closely approach.

Rock iguanas on Little Water Cay may approach quite closely.

Diving Health & Safety

The Turks and Caicos Islands are a generally healthy destination and pose no serious health risks to most visitors. There are no endemic tropical diseases, and no vaccinations are required to enter the country unless you are arriving from a high-risk country. The U.S. Centers for Disease Control & Prevention regularly posts updates on health-related concerns around the world specifically for travelers. For up-to-date regional health information visit their website (www.cdc.gov), or call (toll-free from the U.S.) ☎ 888-232-3299 and request Document 000005 to receive a list of documents available by fax.

The tropical sun is likely to be the biggest risk to the average visitor. Be certain to pack a high-quality sunscreen with a high SPF (sun protection factor) and wear a hat or cover-up when possible. Carry pure aloe vera gel in case you do get sunburned—a liberal application (as much as your skin will absorb) will help prevent blistering and peeling. You may also want to carry a topical antihistamine for relief of any minor irritating stings from marine creatures. Also be sure to drink plenty of water to prevent dehydration. Though most visitors don't have a problem with the water or food here, drinking bottled water is generally a good idea when traveling.

Pre-Trip Preparation

Your general state of health, diving skill level and specific equipment needs are the three most important factors that impact any dive trip. If you honestly assess these before you leave, you'll be well on your way to assuring a safe dive trip.

First, if you're not in shape, start exercising. Second, if you haven't dived for a while (six months is too long) and your skills are rusty, do a local dive with an experienced buddy or take a scuba review course. Finally, inspect your dive gear. Feeling good physically, diving with experience and with reliable equipment will not only increase your safety, but will also enhance your enjoyment underwater.

At least a month before your trip, inspect your dive gear. Remember, your regulator should be serviced annually, whether you've used it or not. If you use a dive computer and can replace the battery yourself, change it before the trip or buy a spare one to take along. Otherwise, send the computer to the manufacturer for a battery replacement.

If possible, find out before you go on the trip if the dive center rents or services the type of gear you own. If not, you might want to take spare parts or even spare gear. A spare mask is always a good idea.

Purchase any additional equipment you might need, such as a dive light and tank marker light for night diving, a line reel for wreck diving, etc. Make sure you have at least a whistle attached to your BC. Better yet, add a marker tube (also known as a safety sausage or come-to-me).

About a week before taking off, do a final check of your gear, grease o-rings, check batteries and assemble a save-a-dive kit. This kit should at minimum contain extra mask and fin straps, snorkel keeper, mouthpiece, valve cap, zip ties and o-rings. Don't forget to pack a first-aid kit and medications such as decongestants, ear drops, antihistamines and motion sickness tablets.

Diving & Flying

Most divers in Turks and Caicos arrive by plane. While it's fine to dive soon *after* flying, it's important to remember that your last dive should be completed at least 24 hours *before* your flight to minimize the risk of decompression sickness, caused by residual nitrogen in the blood.

Medical & Recompression Facilities

The only full-service public hospital is Grand Turk Hospital (☎ 649-946-2233), which has an emergency room but is gloomy. It's considered a last resort by locals, who advise using the private medical centers on Provo: the Associated Medical Practices clinic (☎ 649-946-4242) on Leeward Highway or the New Era Medical Centre in Blue Hills.

For emergency services (ambulance, police or fire) call ☎ 999 or 911. In medical emergencies beyond the capacity of the local hospital, patients are flown by air ambulance to full-service hospitals in Nassau or Miami.

Travelers can also visit the government clinics on each of the islands:

Grand Turk	☎ 649-946-2328
Middle Caicos	☎ 649-946-6145
North Caicos	☎ 649-946-7194
Providenciales	☎ 649-941-3000
South Caicos	☎ 649-946-3216

A government doctor pays a weekly visit to Salt Cay.

The Associated Medical Practices clinic on Provo has a two-person recompression chamber, run by experienced dive doctors. The physicians who run the chamber will assess the need for treatment. Contact the clinic directly if you suspect a problem. However, visitors should be advised that DAN insurance is not accepted in the Turks and Caicos. If you find yourself in need of a "chamber dive," you will have to pay the cost up front (cash or credit card) and then seek reimbursement from your primary health care provider and then from DAN if you are a member.

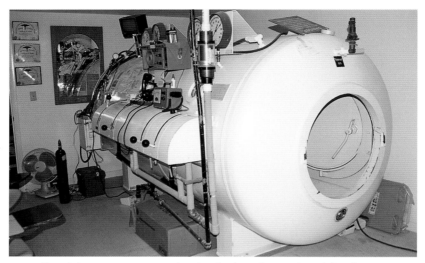

Provo's two-person recompression chamber is run by experienced dive doctors.

DAN

Divers Alert Network (DAN) is an international membership association of individuals and organizations sharing a common interest in diving and safety. It operates a 24-hour diving emergency hotline in the U.S.: ☎ **919-684-8111 or 919-684-4DAN** (-4326). The latter accepts collect calls in a dive emergency. Though DAN does not directly provide medical care, it does provide advice on early treatment, evacuation and hyperbaric treatment of diving-related injuries. Divers should contact DAN for assistance as soon as a diving emergency is suspected.

DAN membership is reasonably priced and includes DAN TravelAssist, a membership benefit that covers medical air evacuation from anywhere in the world for any illness or injury. For a small additional fee, divers can get secondary insurance coverage for decompression illness. For membership details, contact DAN at ☎ 800-446-2671 in the U.S. or ☎ 919-684-2948 elsewhere. DAN can also be reached at www.diversalertnetwork.org.

Diving in the Turks & Caicos

Many experienced divers believe the Turks and Caicos Islands offer the best diving in the Caribbean. They certainly offer a world-class diving experience. Excellent visibility, unspoiled reefs, spectacular vertical walls and an abundance of marine animals both big and small attract divers from around the globe.

Most of the dive sites are wall dives on the protected sides of the islands, away from the prevailing trade winds. The walls here drop below 6,000ft (1,800m) in most places, providing ample opportunities for deep diving, but few sites need to be dived deep to be fully appreciated. Typically, a dive site's most interesting features are above 130ft (40m). The depth ranges included with each dive site description indicate where the site's best features are, and a "+" after the range means deeper dives are possible. Be sure to plan your dives and dive your plans—keep an eye on your depth gauge at these wall sites.

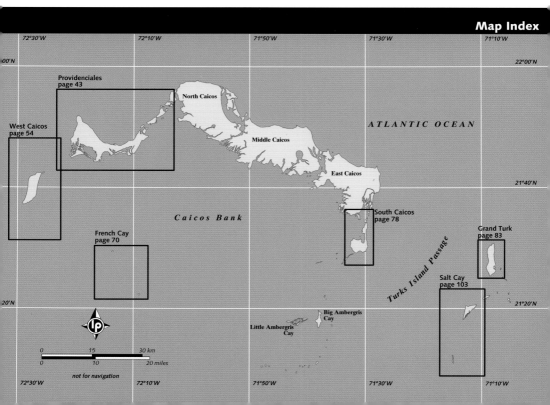

Map Index

Providenciales page 43

North Caicos

West Caicos page 54

Middle Caicos

ATLANTIC OCEAN

East Caicos

Caicos Bank

South Caicos page 78

Grand Turk page 83

French Cay page 70

Turks Island Passage

Salt Cay page 103

72°30'W 72°10'W 71°50'W 71°30'W 71°10'W

22°00'N

21°40'N

21°20'N

20'N

Big Ambergris Cay

Little Ambergris Cay

0   15   30 km
0   10   20 miles

not for navigation

Water temperatures are between 82 and 84°F (28 and 29°C) for most of the year, dropping into the high 70s Fahrenheit (about 26°C) in the winter months. Average visibility ranges from 60 to 120ft (18 to 37m), dictated in part by tides and currents. On the outgoing tide, water is swept off the shallow banks and becomes clouded with silt and plankton, reducing visibility. On the incoming tide, water moves from the deep across the dive sites, bringing clean water and increasing visibility.

Several parts of the Turks and Caicos Islands have become prime dive destinations. Providenciales and Grand Turk have the greatest selection of services, but you can find operators to take you to sites around West Caicos, French Cay, South Caicos, Long Cay and Salt Cay as well.

Almost anywhere you dive, you will find incredibly lush walls providing a tapestry of colors, shapes and textures. Many of the sites offer a treasure trove of interesting and unique invertebrates for macrophotographers. Whether you dive remote sites or those near inhabited areas, schools of tropical fish, sharks, sea turtles, wild dolphins, rays and even humpback whales fill the waters. Divers typically access sites by day boats from a nearby port or by live-aboards. A few excellent shore dives are also available.

Day Boats

Day boat dive operations throughout the Turks and Caicos Islands typically have fast, reliable boats to take small, intimate groups of divers to nearby dive sites, as well as more remote areas.

The day boats out of Provo visit not only the dive sites on the outer edge of Grace Bay and north of Pine Cay, but also the excellent diving on Northwest Point, the western side of West Caicos and even the more remote walls near French Cay. These trips across the shallows of the Caicos Bank range from 30

Day boats are typically small and, on Grand Turk, often pick divers up from shore.

minutes to an hour and a half, depending on the water conditions, speed of the boat and where the operator launches. (Provo day boats operate out of several areas, including Turtle Cove, Leeward Marina and Grace Bay.)

The dive operator in South Caicos visits sites along the east coast of Long Cay and the southern coast of South Caicos, which lie on the western edge of the Turks Island Passage. Though most sites along the south coast of South Caicos can be reached within 20 minutes, trips to sites at the far end of Long Cay can take up to 45 minutes.

On Grand Turk, many of the popular sites are just 300 yards (270m) off the island's western shoreline—and within five to 20 minutes from launch. Salt Cay's operators run trips out of Balfour Town to the region's popular sites, most of which are within 15 minutes from the dock. Because Grand Turk and Salt Cay are so close to one another, operators on either island will make the 40-minute to hour-long trip to the other island.

Live-Aboards

Several live-aboard boats operate out of the Turks and Caicos Islands: the *Turks and Caicos Aggressor* (Turtle Cove, Provo), the Peter Hughes *Sea Dancer* (Turtle Cove, Provo) and the Peter Hughes *Wind Dancer* (Commercial Dock, Grand Turk). Each runs seven-day itineraries, Saturday to Saturday, which allow for five and a half days of diving. Ocean Outback (Sapodilla Bay, Provo) and Tao Live-aboard Charters (Turtle Cove, Provo) also charter boats for live-aboard trips.

The live-aboards out of Provo spend most of their time at West Caicos and Northwest Point, but also dive French Cay when conditions allow. These boats will occasionally make a crossing to South Caicos for a day. The live-aboard out of Grand Turk spends much of the time at sites along the west coasts of Grand Turk and Salt Cay, but also goes to South Caicos and the HMS *Endymion*, south of Salt Cay, when conditions allow.

In the winter months (January to March), the *Turks and Caicos Aggressor* and the Peter Hughes *Wind Dancer* run special humpback whale charters from Grand Turk to the Silver Banks, which are a 10-hour run east of Grand Turk, north of the Dominican Republic.

Snorkeling

Although diving is the primary focus in the Turks and Caicos Islands, many areas offer excellent

Snorkelers can access myriad fish and formations just a few feet from the surface.

snorkeling and free-diving opportunities. Marine life that you rarely find in shallow water—such as lemon sharks, African pompano jacks, loggerhead turtles, eagle rays and nurse sharks—are commonly encountered while snorkeling here.

The mangroves near the northwest end of Providenciales offer opportunities to encounter upside-down jellyfish, flying gurnard, an occasional seahorse and even juvenile blacktip sharks. Just outside Turtle Cove, Smith's Reef offers a chain of lush coral heads that come to within 5ft (2m) of the surface. In this area, snorkelers frequently see southern stingrays, small hawksbill turtles and nurse sharks.

Snorkeling through Provo's mangroves can be quite rewarding.

Tips for Evaluating a Dive Operator

Everyone has their own preferences when it comes to a dive operator, but we all expect some basics, like safety, efficiency and fun. How do you make sure that's what you'll get? Here are some things to look for:

- Is the operation well organized? Is sign-up quick and easy? The best dive operators take you through all the necessary procedures with minimum effort, but don't make you feel like you're on an assembly line.

- Check out the customer amenities. Is parking convenient? Is a comfortable area provided while you wait to board the dive boat? Does the operation have a retail store, and does it stock the gear you might need? Are snacks and beverages available for the trip? Is there a clean gear-rinse and storage area?

- Careful maintenance is a good sign. Are the facilities in good condition? Is the rental gear well maintained and carefully stored? Is the boat clean and reliable?

- Take a peek at the compressor room. Is it well ventilated and clean? Are the tanks in good shape?

- Find out how long the staff has worked there. Staff longevity is good, as it means people are treated well and enjoying their jobs.

- Is everyone having fun? If the customers and staff are having a good time, you probably will too.

Another favorite snorkeling area is next to the ironshore west of West Caicos. Up close and personal meetings with large nurse sharks, schools of reef squid, eagle rays and lemon sharks regularly occur in only 5ft (2m) of water. The shallows around French Cay and at Point Pleasant off the north end of Salt Cay feature magnificent stands of elkhorn coral, as well as spotted eagle rays, giant pufferfish, turtles and small reef sharks.

Grand Turk has two very unique snorkeling areas. Sunray Beach at Gibb's Cay, on the southeast side of Grand Turk, offers a very close encounter with large southern stingrays. These rays will actually come up to the waterline to greet visitors as they wade into the water. A snorkel or free-dive trip along Governor's Beach and the nearby South Dock area is also an incredible experience. Here snorkelers will find seahorses, shortnose batfish, golden shrimp, scorpionfish, moray eels, octopuses, nudibranchs, flying gurnards, southern stingrays and even an occasional manta ray.

You can rent underwater scooters at some of the more popular beach destinations.

Certification & Specialty Courses

It would be difficult to find an environment that is more conducive to getting your Open Water dive certification than the Turks and Caicos Islands. Whether you finish your class work at home and complete just the checkout dive in the islands or come to do an all-inclusive certification class, the Turks and Caicos are definitely the way to go for the beginning diver. Protected reefs, lush corals and sponges, beautiful tropical fish and many big and interesting animals are just part of the package. The local dive operators have friendly, professional instructors who not only know their business, but also leave their students with a yearning to do more.

However, the Turks and Caicos are not just a great place for novice divers. The live-aboards and land-based operators also offer advanced technical certifications and many specialty classes. A visit to the Turks and Caicos is a great opportunity to earn advanced diving certification and learn new skills, such as nitrox, rebreathers (closed as well as semiclosed) and even the use of mixed gases. Contact the *Turks and Caicos Aggressor*, Peter Hughes Diving Inc. (*Wind Dancer* and *Sea Dancer*), Big Blue or the other operators for class details. Excellent photography classes for all skill levels are offered by Fish Frames in Provo and by the aforementioned live-aboard dive boat operators.

Dive Site Icons

The symbols at the beginning of each dive site description provide a quick summary of some of the important characteristics of each site:

 Good snorkeling or free-diving site.

 Remains or partial remains of a wreck can be seen at this site.

 Sheer wall or drop-off.

 Deep dive. Features of this dive are found in water deeper than 90ft (27m).

 Strong currents may be encountered at this site.

 Strong surge (the horizontal movement of water caused by waves) may be encountered at this site.

 Shore dive. This site can be accessed from shore.

 Caves or caverns are a prominent feature of this site. Only experienced cave divers should explore inner cave areas.

 Marine preserve. Special protective regulations apply in this area.

Pisces Rating System for Dives & Divers

The dive sites in this book are rated according to the following diver skill-level rating system. These are not absolute ratings but apply to divers at a particular time, diving at a particular place. For instance, someone unfamiliar with prevailing conditions might be considered a novice diver at one dive area, but an intermediate diver at another, more familiar location.

Novice: A novice diver should be accompanied by an instructor, divemaster or advanced diver on all dives. A novice diver generally fits the following profile:
◆ basic scuba certification from an internationally recognized certifying agency
◆ dives infrequently (less than one trip a year)
◆ logged fewer than 25 total dives
◆ little or no experience diving in similar waters and conditions
◆ dives no deeper than 60ft (18m)

Intermediate: An intermediate diver generally fits the following profile:
◆ may have participated in some form of continuing diver education
◆ logged between 25 and 100 dives
◆ dives no deeper than 130ft (40m)
◆ has been diving in similar waters and conditions within the last six months

Advanced: An advanced diver generally fits the following profile:
◆ advanced certification
◆ has been diving for more than two years and logged over 100 dives
◆ has been diving in similar waters and conditions within the last six months

Regardless of your skill level, you should be in good physical condition and know your limitations. If you are uncertain of your own level of expertise for a particular site, ask the advice of a local dive instructor. He or she is best qualified to assess your abilities based on the site's prevailing dive conditions. Ultimately, however, you must decide if you are capable of making a particular dive, a decision that should take into account your level of training, recent experience and physical condition, as well as the conditions at the site. Remember that conditions can change at any time, even during a dive.

Providenciales Dive Sites

Providenciales, or Provo, is the center of the Turks and Caicos' economic activity and is where you'll find most of the country's world-class resorts. Though once known to only a handful of wealthy foreigners, the island has experienced a recent growth spurt and now boasts travelers' amenities in a wide range of prices.

Provo is approximately 14 miles (23km) long, ranges from 1 to 4 miles (2 to 6km) wide and offers an incredible 12-mile (19km) stretch of white-sand beach. Popular activities include parasailing, windsurfing, horseback riding, hiking and kayaking, as well as scuba diving and snorkeling. The island's three diving and snorkeling areas are Pine Cay, Grace Bay and Northwest Point.

Pine Cay is a small, 800-acre privately owned island off Provo's northeast end, just east of Little Water Cay. The dive sites—underwater seamounts that rise to within 50ft (15m) of the surface—are all on the north side of the cay.

Grace Bay, on Provo's north side, is protected from tradewinds for most of the year. It is bordered by a 14-mile-long (23km-long) barrier reef. To the east, a massive spur-and-groove fringe reef runs roughly southwest to northeast outside the barrier reef. The top of the barrier reef is fairly shallow, between 25 and 40ft (8 and 12m). A series of interesting dives lies where the steep mini-wall slopes to the sandy bottom 100 to 120ft (30 to 37m) below.

You'll find more than a dozen sites at Northwest Point, along Provo's leeward side, where a vertical wall provides 3 miles (5km) of exceptional wall-diving opportunities. These wall dives are well known for their magnificent formations of purple and yellow tube sponges and elephant ear sponges. These sites all fall within the Northwest Point Marine National Park.

Provo's Grace Bay is a popular resort area with a multitude of aquatic activities.

Live-aboard boats leave from Turtle Cove, and day boats leave from a variety of ports, including Turtle Cove, Leeward Marina and Grace Bay.

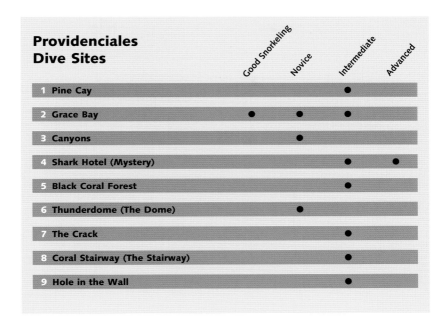

Providenciales Dive Sites	Good Snorkeling	Novice	Intermediate	Advanced
1 Pine Cay			●	
2 Grace Bay	●	●	●	
3 Canyons		●		
4 Shark Hotel (Mystery)			●	●
5 Black Coral Forest			●	
6 Thunderdome (The Dome)		●		
7 The Crack			●	
8 Coral Stairway (The Stairway)			●	
9 Hole in the Wall			●	

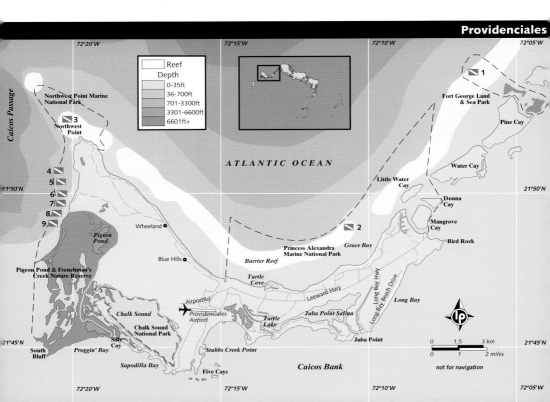

Providenciales

1 Pine Cay

You'll find several worthwhile dive sites along Pine Cay's north shore. The mooring for **Football Field** is in 50ft at the top of a steep slope that drops down to a flat sand bottom at 130ft. This site is in the Fort George Land and Sea Park. The top of the reef is a typical spur-and-groove formation with an extensive crevice and massive coral canyons. Many fish school

Location: NE of Provo

Depth Range: 35-130ft (11-40m)

Access: Boat

Expertise Rating: Intermediate

in this area, including snappers, jacks, tangs, barracuda, black durgeons and chubs. Other diverse tropical fish commonly seen here include groupers, parrotfish and angelfish.

Eagle Ray Pass, just west of Football Field, is also generally considered to be in the Fort George Land and Sea Park. A sandy gully leads divers down to a sloping wall between 35 and 70ft deep. This Pine Cay site is well known for pelagics such as eagle rays and sharks, which swim through the nearby Fort George Cut. The healthy assortment of hard corals includes both brain and star corals.

Divers will see angelfish throughout the Turks and Caicos.

2 Grace Bay

This area is an excellent novice dive, as well as a warm-up site for more experienced divers to use before heading off to the more remote sites. A signed snorkeling trail is offshore at Grace Bay, but well inside the barrier reef.

You'll find the bay's best dive sites (**Graceland**, **Pinnacles** and **Cathedral**) outside of the Club Med Cut. A friendly

Location: NE shore of Provo

Depth Range: 25-120ft (8-37m)

Access: Boat

Expertise Rating: Novice (inside reef)
Intermediate (outside reef)

5ft barracuda and a bulky Nassau grouper cruise between these sites. Divers will regularly see small Caribbean reef sharks off the wall, as well as turtles in the shallows and in the deep cuts that run through the buttress reef. The endless assortment of tropical fish includes parrotfish, angelfish, butterflyfish, filefish and many others. The reef surface is adorned with pillar corals, giant brain corals and sea rods.

Permanent moorings have been placed at **Sunset Strip**, **2 Sharks**, **Crocodile**, **Coral Gables**, **Graceland** and **Grouper Hole**. Some excellent sites lie farther west, just outside Turtle Cove, including **Aquarium** (with a permanent mooring), **Southwest Wreck** and **Shark Hole**. All of these sites are within the boundaries of the Princess Alexandra Marine National Park.

JoJo the dolphin makes frequent appearances in Grace Bay, often following dive boats out to the sites and interacting with divers. Two other dolphins, dubbed Misty and Sunshine, have also started showing up at sites around Provo and West Caicos. These dolphins have acquired the strange habit of picking up pieces of coral and sponges and passing them between themselves and to divers.

JoJo the Dolphin

JoJo is Provo's resident 7ft (2m) male Atlantic bottlenose dolphin. He left his pod and lives in the shallow waters of Grace Bay and Pine Cay. Since 1980 he has regularly interacted with divers and snorkelers.

The friendly interactions between JoJo and humans have attracted much worldwide attention. It is said that when he first appeared he was shy, limiting his contact with humans to following or playing in the bow waves of boats. Over the years he has become extremely gregarious, seeking out human playmates.

He is now so popular that he has been named a national treasure by the Ministry of Natural Resources. JoJo has his own warden, who studies his behavior and looks out for him as part of the JoJo Dolphin Project. For more information contact ☎/fax 649-941-5617; P.O. Box 153, Providenciales, Turks and Caicos, BWI, www.jojo.tc.

3 Canyons

Canyons is the northernmost dive site on Provo's northwest point. It is actually well away from the wall (between the drop-off and the shoreline). Because of its proximity to the point and Caicos Passage, the site regularly experiences a moderate current. Though Canyons is generally suitable for novice divers, when the

Location: N of Northwest Point

Depth Range: 40-70ft (12-21m)

Access: Boat or live-aboard

Expertise Rating: Novice

Giant sea plumes decorate the tops of the channels at Canyons.

current is strong, this site is for intermediate and advanced divers only. Visibility can be 100ft, but silt and sediment carried by the current sometimes reduces visibility to less than 40ft.

The terrain here is a series of canyons, ravines and channels. The tops of these channels are lined with assorted soft corals, such as sea fans, rods, whips and sea plumes—species that thrive where there is a lot of water movement. The sides of the channels are lined with hard corals, including plate and star corals, which form small caves and recesses.

You will find many caves, arches and swim-throughs to explore. Although this area is not teeming with marine life, an interesting assortment of larger animals, such as nurse sharks and turtles, reside here. Look for lobsters, large dog snappers and groupers tucked away out of the current.

As you explore this area, you never know what you will run into around the next corner. Photographers should be ready for the opportunity to frame these critters within the terrain's natural features, such as arches and cave openings.

4 Shark Hotel (Mystery)

Shark Hotel was named by Art Pickering of Provo Turtle Divers, though it is also referred to as Mystery by several dive operators. As is often the case when "shark" is part of a site's name, you won't find many sharks at the site. It may be that when this site was originally named, there were frequent encounters with nurse sharks, found tucked away in holes in the reef. The most interesting areas of this spectacular deep dive are between 90 and 130ft.

Location: Northwest Point Marine National Park

Depth Range: 40-130ft+ (12-40m+)

Access: Boat or live-aboard

Expertise Rating:
Intermediate (on the plateau)
Advanced (deep wall)

You'll find two walls here. The first is a mini-wall beginning at about 45ft that drops off fairly steeply to 80ft, where a wide ledge or plateau extends outward and runs for several hundred yards along the wall. The plateau slopes gradually from the base of the mini-wall to a vertical drop-off at 110ft. Along the plateau at about 90ft, divers can enter a chimney that exits the wall at about 135 or 140ft. Just north of this exit is a large canyon that you can follow back up to about 80ft. The current through here is minimal, and the visibility is usually quite good.

The plateau and walls are adorned with a nice variety of corals and sponges, including black coral, wire coral, barrel sponges, colorful tube sponges, rope sponges, vase sponges and plate coral. Don't forget to keep an eye toward the blue water (as well as on your depth gauge), where divers will see schools of horse-eye jacks and an occasional Caribbean reef shark or black-tip shark off the deep wall. Schools of ocean triggerfish and jacks hang out around the plateau.

At the top of the mini-wall at 45ft you'll find small schools of grunts, snappers and goatfish that congregate during the day. At night these fish split up and forage for food atop the sand flats.

Perched on the back reef at about 40ft and not far from the mooring, you'll find several huge stands of pillar coral, one of

Trumpetfish can grow more than 3ft long.

which rises about 12ft from the bottom—it is perhaps the largest in the Turks and Caicos Islands. Use a wide-angle lens to photograph divers beside pillar coral to show the coral's size. Concentrate on shooting at slightly upward angles to obtain dramatic images.

Check out the many cleaning stations in this area, where a line of assorted fish wait patiently to be groomed by cleaner shrimp and gobies. Fish that are preoccupied with being cleaned often allow divers to approach closely, creating great photo opportunities.

5 Black Coral Forest

Black Coral Forest's main attraction is a spectacular vertical wall that tops out between 45 and 50ft. The wall itself bottoms out at about 130ft on a sloping, silty, sandy bottom, which in turn becomes a sheer wall at 200ft.

A chimney at the northern end of this site begins at about 55ft and opens out along the shallower of these walls at

Location: Northwest Point Marine National Park

Depth Range: 45-110ft+ (14-34m+)

Access: Boat or live-aboard

Expertise Rating: Intermediate

Dense stands of black coral grow along the wall at this aptly named site.

about 90ft. The center of the wall offers a protruding buttress covered with large red deepwater sea fans. A vertical crevice just to the south of this buttress offers four different species of black corals, including long strands of wire corals.

The southern section of the site is perhaps the most beautiful. The best diving is between 45 and 90ft, with a few features down to 110ft. A long undercut area on the wall offers tightly packed bundles of colorful rope sponges, including dense tangles of red rope sponges. Bring a light to explore the interior of this depression. Look closely for an amazing assortment of tiny camouflaged invertebrates and small fish.

Beneath the southern end of this undercut area at about 95ft, you'll find a healthy, round, bright orange elephant ear sponge. Just a bit farther south along the wall a much larger elephant ear protrudes from an alcove at about 80ft. Pair the elephant ear sponges, barrel sponges or deepwater gorgonians with a diver for dramatic wide-angle photographs.

The back reef in this area is relatively uninteresting. However, some nice stands of elkhorn corals grow in the shallower areas closer to the beach. Though the top of the wall has a fairly thin coral veneer, it supports a nice variety of tropical fish. Divers will almost always see large pufferfish, the ever-present queen triggerfish, barracuda, large trumpetfish, moray eels and southern stingrays.

6 Thunderdome (The Dome)

You'll find The Dome inshore of the wall at Northwest Point. This was once the site of a French television game show. Abandoned tiki huts that were used in the show are still visible on the shoreline. Contestants were compelled to free-dive through a rectangular opening in the top of the dome and ask for air from one of several "mermaids" equipped with air tanks and an octopus regulator. If you asked the wrong one for air, you received only a breath or two and had to swim like mad for the surface. The show was cancelled after several contestants suffered air embolisms and had to go to the local recompression chamber.

Location: Northwest Point Marine National Park

Depth Range: 30-40ft+ (9-12m+)

Access: Boat or live-aboard

Expertise Rating: Novice

The dome itself is a large, heavy, steel-mesh structure that sits upright on a flat sand bottom in about 35 or 40ft of water. A couple of sections of the dome have fallen off the structure, leaving one side open and easy to penetrate. A

Divers investigate Thunderdome's outer shell.

A whitespotted filefish makes its exit from the dome.

lot of friendly tropical fish wander in and out of the dome. Many of the holes are too small to accommodate the queen angelfish, pairs of gray angelfish, whitespotted filefish and scrawled filefish that come in to feed on algae and encrusting sponges. As a result, divers are often able to get very close to fish that are usually too skittish to capture on film.

The Dome is also considered Northwest Point's best night dive. Macro subjects too numerous to count include neck crabs, octopuses, nudibranchs, flamingo tongues, fingerprint cyphomas, rough fileclams and tube worms.

The entire back reef area near the dome comprises a series of low-profile spur-and-groove coral ridges with sand channels. The top of the nearby wall is at about 50ft. This area is referred to as **The Chimney** because of the vertical shaft that begins at 50ft and opens at 75ft along the vertical wall. A steep sandy slope ends at the lip of another drop-off at 200ft.

Thunderdome truly offers many options for photographers. Portraits of fish, divers with fish, divers peeking through portholes and, of course, macro shots are among the favorites.

A diver looks through a porthole in the dome.

7 The Crack

The Crack, found along the wall at Northwest Point, derives its name from the steep crevice that cuts through the reef buttress from the top of the wall at about 50ft down to about 100ft. As you approach the wall, the crevice angles to the left slightly, running to the southwest.

Location: Northwest Point Marine National Park

Depth Range: 50-120ft+ (15-37m+)

Access: Boat or live-aboard

Expertise Rating: Intermediate

As you swim through the crack toward the wall, look on the right-hand side for the large anemone just above a healthy barrel sponge at a depth of about 85ft. Their position on the wall allows you to photograph them together with divers and a blue-water background.

This vertical wall's jagged face weaves in and out, offering large undercuts. Inside these depressions you may find lobster, Nassau groupers and flowing schools of silversides. The numerous large, healthy barrel sponges are excellent photo subjects. The wall is literally covered with long corkscrew wire corals. Look closely for the gobies and shrimp that hang out on these corals. Tangles of rope sponges are tucked into many of the fissures. You will also find several large purple tube sponges protruding from the wall. Divers may occasionally encounter a reef shark or eagle ray in this vicinity.

The top of the reef is fairly flat with a low-profile strip reef at the lip of the drop-off. Schools of snappers and schoolmasters congregate along the edge. The back reef has low-profile ridges and small coral heads scattered amid the sand-and-rubble bottom.

The permanent mooring is northeast of the crack at about 40ft. Marine life around the mooring includes queen triggerfish, southern stingrays, angelfish, parrotfish and sand tilefish.

Lobsters hide in depressions along The Crack's coral fringe.

8 Coral Stairway (The Stairway)

The top of Northwest Point's wall is fairly deep at this site—starting between 60 and 80ft. As you move away from the top of the drop-off, a series of coral buttresses gets progressively deeper, like a giant stairway. The reef is formed of densely packed hard corals. Soft corals, including sea rods, fans and whips, are abundant. A chimney structure drops downward at the end of one of the cuts in the wall.

Location: Northwest Point Marine National Park

Depth Range: 60-120ft+ (18-37m+)

Access: Boat or live-aboard

Expertise Rating: Intermediate

Though this site isn't particularly colorful, you'll find a lot of healthy barrel sponges, brown antler sponges and brown tube sponges. Schools of snappers, Atlantic spadefish and grunts are common. Divers may encounter tiger and Nassau groupers, and eagle rays are seen fairly regularly. Lots of black durgeons, butterflyfish, angelfish, orange-spotted filefish, parrotfish, hamlets and trumpetfish flit around the reef at The Stairway's top steps. This a good area to take close-up fish portraits.

Trumpetfish shadow other fish while hunting in the shallows.

9 Hole in the Wall

Hole in the Wall is the southernmost dive site along Northwest Point's wall. The site is named after a large opening at about 55ft in the top of the reef. This hole leads to a partially open chimney structure. The chimney is pretty narrow, so before you swim through, check that your octopus regulator and gauges aren't dangling. Also, be careful with your fins

Location: Northwest Point Marine National Park

Depth Range: 40-90ft+ (12-27m+)

Access: Boat or live-aboard

Expertise Rating: Intermediate

to prevent stirring up sediment or damaging the sponges, corals and other invertebrates that inhabit the interior of the chimney.

The lip of the wall is rounded between 50 and 90ft, then drops sheerly into the abyss. The wall, which largely consists of immense sheets of plate corals and other hard corals, is split by several deep cuts. The sheets of plate coral on the wall give it a terraced effect.

Schools of grunts and snappers float or drift about at the top of the wall. Watch the schools to see where they hang out before you try to approach for photographs—even when they are disturbed, they will return to the same area once they are used to your presence. Position yourself in a spot that allows you to frame the fish next to a coral head or soft coral plume. If you are patient, they will swim back into your picture.

You will also find quite a few barracuda hovering around the reef. If you peek into depressions under the coral heads, you will find spotted eels and maybe a large green moray eel.

The mooring is in about 40ft of water. Scattered coral heads and patch reefs decorate the shallow areas.

Large barracuda often hover over the reef.

West Caicos Dive Sites

West Caicos is an uninhabited island 10 miles (16km) southwest of Providenciales. The island sits at the western edge of the Caicos Bank. The interior of the island is legally protected by the Lake Catherine Nature Reserve, and most of the reefs along the west shoreline are legally protected by the West Caicos Marine National Park.

Almost all of the dive sites at West Caicos are perched on the edge of the wall that runs only 100 to 150 yards (90 to 135m) offshore for the entire 6-mile (10km) length of the island's west coast. Diving conditions here are almost always calm—the prevailing winds come from the southeast or northeast, so sites are protected by the island's landmass. This region is easily accessible by live-aboards or day boats from Providenciales.

The wall diving here is spectacular. The top of the wall is between 35 and 55ft (11 and 17m), while the mostly vertical drop-off plummets to 6,000ft (1,800m). Huge barrel sponges, magnificent deepwater sea fans, large elephant ear sponges, five different types of black corals and healthy hard corals occupy the face of the wall. You'll spot reef sharks on almost every dive.

At night, horse-eye jacks and black jacks chase schools of smaller fish in and out of the light below the boat, while eels and octopuses hunt for prey on the bottom. Interesting and unique invertebrates, including squid, cowries, crabs and shrimp, reward night divers who focus on the concentrated area within the beam of their lights.

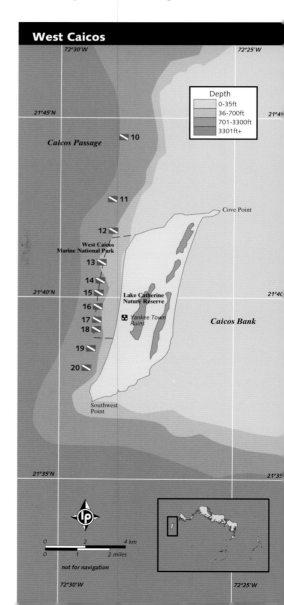

West Caicos

72°30'W   72°25'W

Depth
0-35ft
36-700ft
701-3300ft
3301ft+

21°45'N   21°45'

Caicos Passage   ⬛ 10

⬛ 11

Cove Point

12 ⬛
West Caicos
Marine National Park

13 ⬛

14 ⬛

21°40'N   15 ⬛   21°40'
Lake Catherine
16 ⬛   Nature Reserve

17 ⬛   ⊠ Yankee Town   Caicos Bank
18 ⬛   Ruins

19 ⬛

20 ⬛

Southwest
Point

21°35'N   21°35'

0   2   4 km
0   1   2 miles
not for navigation

72°30'W   72°25'W

The shallows along the ironshore offer some superb snorkeling. Dive boats may visit sites on the backside (southeastern side of West Caicos) when an unusual weather front comes from the north or northwest.

The west coast of West Caicos is weathered limestone ironshore.

West Caicos Dive Sites

	Good Snorkeling	Novice	Intermediate	Advanced
10 Tons of Sponges		●		
11 Land of the Giants			●	
12 Midnight Manta		●		
13 Highway to Heaven	●		●	
14 Elephant Ear Canyon			●	
15 The Gully			●	
16 Boat Cove (Rock Garden Interlude)	●	●		
17 Driveway (Yankee Town)	●	●		
18 Brandywine (Brandy-Glass Sponge)	●	●		
19 White Face (The Anchor)	●	●		
20 Sunday Service	●	●		

10 Tons of Sponges

If you guessed that Tons of Sponges is named for its tremendous diversity of porifera, you'd be right. For colorful and immobile photo subjects, this site can't be beat.

The lip of the drop-off is 30 to 35ft deep. This wall dive at the west end of the Sandbore Channel is bordered by two sloping promontories that extend to the west, away from the wall, roughly forming a crescent shape. Inside the northern edge of this crescent you'll find some beautiful fluorescent-purple azure vase sponges and many large deepwater gorgonians between 60 and 100ft.

The south side of the crescent is one of the best areas to see all kinds of large sponges. Among the incredible variety of sponges are branching vase, azure vase, brown bowl, netted barrel, leathery barrel, touch-me-not, rope, encrusting, yellow tube and many others.

Location: 2 miles (3km) N of West Caicos

Depth Range: 30-100ft+ (9-30m+)

Access: Boat or live-aboard

Expertise Rating: Novice

Lobsters and octopuses are frequently seen here out in the open during the day. Keep your eyes out for Caribbean reef sharks, which occasionally cruise in and out of this area.

The currents here can be quite strong. Visibility is also highly variable (ranging from 30 to 100ft) and is dependent upon the tides and weather. You'll get the best visibility when the weather is calm, and on an incoming tide until a couple hours after high tide.

Prolific Porifera

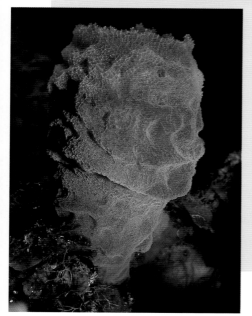

A wide variety of sponges (phylum Porifera, meaning hole-bearing) are common throughout the Turks and Caicos' waters. The most common types are vase, rope and barrel sponges—some of which can grow to over 6ft (2m). The Turks and Caicos Islands also have an unusually high number of elephant ear and antler sponges, as well as a few azure vase sponges (pictured at left).

Sponges draw water, containing food and oxygen, into their interior through small holes called incurrent pores found all over the sponge. Once inside, the water is then pumped through the sponge tissue by the movement of whiplike extensions called flagella. At the same time, nutrients and oxygen are filtered out of the water into the sponge. The water then moves into the interior cavity and exits the sponge via one or more excurrent openings.

11 Land of the Giants

The wall here tops out between 40 and 45ft and slopes down to about 70ft, where an extensive undercut section extends downward and bottoms out on a sand-covered shelf at about 140ft. The wall is covered with hard corals, including star corals and plate corals. It is also decorated with massive sponges—huge barrel sponges, long purple tube sponges and vase sponges—and supports many large black-coral trees, deepwater sea fans and colorful encrusting sponges. Divers will frequently see large animals, including sharks, eagle rays and jacks.

Location: ½ mile (1km) N of West Caicos

Depth Range: 40-110ft+ (12-34m+)

Access: Boat or live-aboard

Expertise Rating: Intermediate

The top of the wall is fairly sparsely covered with coral. However, you'll find many beautiful azure vase sponges near the top of the fringing reef. The northwest section of West Caicos is one of the few places in the Turks and Caicos where these beautiful sponges grow. This reef is also home to Nassau groupers, large porcupine fish, gray angelfish and queen angelfish, most of which are encountered at and near the top of the wall.

Heavy tidal currents occur at this site. On an outgoing tide, the current sweeps around the northern end of the island, bringing silt, nutrients and plankton from the shallow banks. It is best to dive here on an incoming tide (and up to two hours past high tide) to get the best possible visibility and the least amount of current.

Deepwater sea fans flourish in clear water with some current.

12 Midnight Manta

The site was named years ago by Everett Freitas after he encountered mantas on several successive dives. Other divers also reported seeing a 10ft manta on night dives in this area. Unfortunately it has been some time since mantas have been encountered here.

Location: West wall

Depth Range: 60-120ft+ (18-37m+)

Access: Boat or live-aboard

Expertise Rating: Novice

The top of the wall is at about 50ft and slopes gradually (by West Caicos standards) beyond 130ft. Divers are likely to see green morays, lobsters, large spider crabs and nurse sharks tucked away in the coral's recesses.

Octopuses assume a nearly endless variety of shapes and colors.

This is one of several excellent night dives on West Caicos. The back reef is relatively flat, with sand channels and lush coral heads. Crabs, octopuses and lobsters are seen on most dives, during both the day and night. You are likely to see an unusually large number of shrimp, including Pederson shrimp, spotted cleaner shrimp and red night shrimp. Pederson shrimp on corkscrew anemones make for particularly striking photographs.

13 Highway to Heaven

The "highway" of this site is a steeply sloping sand chute that cuts a swath through the fringing reef. The chute narrows to a small gap at the bottom of the slope, where it exits the wall at a depth of 85ft. A plaque on the north side of this gap memorializes the death of a Club Med dive guide. Highway to Heaven was one of her favorite dives and is a fitting tribute.

Location: West wall

Depth Range: 60-120ft+ (18-37m+)

Access: Boat or live-aboard

Expertise Rating: Intermediate

This is one of the deeper wall dives along the west coast of the island. The top of the fringing reef is between 60 and 70ft. The sand chutes abut massive coral heads and coral buttresses between 65 and 100ft deep. Lush hard and soft corals cover the lip of the drop-off and decorate the sides of the sand chutes.

The wall itself is adorned with barrel sponges, black coral, gorgonians and sea whips, but it is somewhat monochromatic. An archway at about 100ft at the end of one of the site's sand chutes is large enough to swim through. Sharks, eagle rays and a variety of other pelagics are usually seen off this deep wall.

The back reef is a vast sand flat with an endless field of garden eels. However, close to the shoreline you'll find some great snorkeling. Lots of healthy sea fans wave gently in the surge. The coves' scalloped undercuts, ravines and shallow caves provide for endless exploration.

Caribbean reef sharks cruise the wall at Highway to Heaven.

14 Elephant Ear Canyon

This site was named for the giant elephant ear sponge that used to occupy a depression at 95ft against the south wall of the main canyon. This bright orange sponge measured more than 10ft by 10ft—the largest known sponge in the Turks and Caicos Islands. Unfortunately, it was slowly smothered under massive amounts of silt.

Location: West wall

Depth Range: 60-100ft+ (18-30m+)

Access: Boat or live-aboard

Expertise Rating: Intermediate

Despite the absence of the sponge, this is still a great dive. The canyon itself begins at the top of the wall in about 60ft of water and opens up to a wider sand chute. The sides of the canyon are composed of thick coral buttresses. The north side offers diverse hard corals, gorgonians and sponges, which are especially prolific between 70 and 100ft deep.

The top of the wall has a low fringing reef at 60ft, cut by several smaller sand chutes. The vertical wall in this area is not straight, but is a series of doglegs, or sharp bends, with undercuts that are stuffed with rope sponges and a variety of black coral. Quite a number of large barrel sponges grow in the sand chutes, as well as out on the wall. Have a wide-angle lens ready to catch pelagics cruising along the wall.

The back reef consists largely of a white sandy bottom devoid of coral heads, but home to colonies of garden eels, as well as stingrays, peacock flounders and queen conch.

The current at this site is usually light, flowing north or south along the wall, depending upon the tides. Along the wall, divers will find a large black coral tree, as well as large tube sponges. Resident marine life includes horse-eye jacks, spadefish, turtles, groupers and schools of goatfish and margates. A resident Caribbean reef shark may appear out of nowhere—it often comes in and circles divers for a better look.

Peacock flounder blend in with the sandy bottom.

15 The Gully

The Gully is primarily a deep dive along a wall formed by a fringing reef. The back reef slopes gradually to a vertical drop-off at 55 or 60ft, which plummets to beyond 6,000ft. A wide variety of soft corals, deepwater gorgonians, barrel sponges and black corals are especially abundant along the lip of the vertical drop-off and down to 115ft.

The site's namesake is a jagged crevasse with a sloping sandy bottom that cuts through the reef. Where the gully exits along the drop-off, the wall's face has a narrow vertical cut 55ft deep at the top and about 85ft deep at the bottom.

As you swim through the gully to the wall, you'll pass two large branches of weedy black coral at about 70ft. Also look for bigeyes, silversides and a large green moray in the recesses as you swim through the gully.

North of where the gully exits onto the wall, you'll see a pair of very large barrel sponges, as well as a photogenic

Location: West wall

Depth Range: 50-115ft (15-35m)

Access: Boat or live-aboard

Expertise Rating: Intermediate

elephant ear sponge with a protuberance that bears a strong resemblance to the Muppet character Gonzo's big hooked nose. Below the cut in the wall, look for the beautiful azure vase sponge at approximately 115ft.

Just south of the main cut and along the wall at 95ft, you'll find a 100ft-wide, 40ft-high alcove that has a relatively flat sandy bottom. Its exaggerated undercut walls are covered with encrusting sponges and algae, as well as large rope and barrel sponges. A large black coral tree, a very healthy elephant ear sponge and a massive purple tube sponge also decorate the space, as well as a few particularly

Barrel sponges and black corals adorn The Gully's sides.

thick and colorful (red, lavender and gray) clusters of rope sponges.

A little farther south, a section of the reef juts from the wall at about 90 to 100ft. This area of the wall has some excellent deepwater gorgonians and large barrel sponges. The colorful sponges and gorgonians on the wall between 80 and 120ft are among your best opportunities to get wide-angle images. Be sure to include a diver in the shot for added perspective.

The mooring is on the back reef at 40ft, amid a scattering of small coral heads. Cleaning stations are common in this area. Marine life includes schools of snappers, schoolmasters and grunts, tiger and Nassau groupers, permits, margates and goatfish. Other tropicals include cowfish, gray and French angelfish and bigeyes.

The shallow area is packed with macro subjects, such as colonial feather duster worms, flamingo tongues, rough file-clams and Christmas tree worms. Just north of the mooring, look for a large club anemone with an assortment of shrimp. Poke around the sea fans and

Dolphin Encounters

A dolphin may invite you to play catch with a shell or piece of tube sponge.

Provo isn't the only place divers might see dolphins in the water. Pods of dolphins are occasionally seen off the West Caicos wall. Author Steve Rosenberg gives an account of his encounters.

"I was coming back to the boat after a dive at The Gully when two bottlenose dolphins buzzed me in about 30ft of water. They rooted around in the sand for a minute and then swam over to me. One of the dolphins had a conch shell in its mouth, which it 'threw' in my direction as it passed. I let the shell drop to the bottom. The dolphin came back, picked up the shell and again swam over and dropped it in front of me. When I continued to play a passive, spectator role, the dolphins seemed to lose interest and swam away, taking their conch shell with them.

"Days later a small pod of dolphins appeared off the back of the *Aggressor* while it was anchored at White Face. A few of us grabbed our masks, fins, snorkels and cameras and jumped in to see if the dolphins would want to play. A pair of dolphins appeared to be tearing at something in a section of the reef. The next thing I knew, I was face to face with the pair, one of which had a piece of tube sponge dangling from its mouth. They proceeded to play catch between themselves, as if showing me what to do with the sponge. Again, one dropped the sponge near me. This time I grabbed the sponge and flicked it back in the direction of the closest dolphin. We engaged in this game of catch for a few minutes, and then the pair moved on to others in our group. I suppose they have trained quite a few divers over the years."

sea rods to reveal a variety of interesting animals, such as slender filefish and decorator crabs.

Encounters with pelagics are fairly common at this site, but you should be first in the water if you want to get a glimpse—some pelagics, including eagle rays and sharks, will become spooked and disappear as more divers enter the water. It is not uncommon to see Caribbean reef sharks, eagle rays, horse-eye jacks, barracuda and black jacks.

16 Boat Cove (Rock Garden Interlude)

This site along the West Caicos wall is particularly lush and colorful. Though commonly referred to as Boat Cove, it resembles a garden of coral and sponges, so it is also called Rock Garden Interlude. The wall has a terrific assortment of large sponges, including long purple tube sponges, barrel sponges, bright orange elephant ear sponges, azure vase sponges and rope sponges, as well as many of the more rare antler sponges.

Location: West wall

Depth Range: 40-130ft+ (12-40m+)

Access: Boat or live-aboard

Expertise Rating: Novice

The reeftop is fairly flat and slopes gently from the mooring (at about 40ft) to the top of the wall. The back reef is composed of scattered coral heads perched on wide expanses of sand. This shallow area inside the mooring offers an excellent opportunity to take photos of queen triggerfish, angelfish, squirrelfish and other tropical fish that congregate near the scattered coral heads.

A sand chute divides the reeftop into north and south sections. Look for the large anemone that lives at the very end of the sand chute. The wall south of the chute offers many large barrel sponges amid lush corals, including sea whips, fans and black coral trees.

On the north side of the sand chute the wall takes a 90° turn, forming a natural promontory. The top of this point slopes down to 65 or 70ft. During an outgoing tide this area generates some exciting fish activity in the current that washes off the nearshore shelf. Divers will frequently encounter reef sharks, turtles, jacks, rainbow runners and other pelagics just off the wall.

Though nocturnal, many species of squirrelfish are seen on the reef during the day.

17 Driveway (Yankee Town)

You'll find this site just south of the Yankee Town ruins. Driveway's back reef features scattered coral heads in 35 to 40ft of water. Quite a number of juvenile drums dance a figure-eight ballet in protected hollows near these coral heads. In the shallows look for sun anemones (4- to 6-inch flattened roundish discs), which usually live in depths between 2 and 10ft, out in the open on the hardpan. You'll find many types of shrimp, including squat anemone shrimp, on these anemones or hiding under their extended arms. The more common types of tropicals seen in this area are Spanish grunts, longspine squirrelfish, queen triggerfish, parrotfish, angelfish and a variety of butterflyfish.

This site is named after the wide sandy chute that cuts through the fringing reef and slopes downward from 50ft at the top of the wall. As the sand chute drops, it forms an inverted "Y" with a plateau isolated between the two branching channels. This massive coral plateau slopes from 80 to 110ft before dropping vertical-

Location: West wall

Depth Range: 35-110ft+ (11-34m+)

Access: Boat or live-aboard

Expertise Rating: Novice

ly. The plateau is covered with layers of plate corals and large formations of star corals. The sides of the sand chutes bend outward, wrapping around the plateau as the wall extends to the north and south.

The vertical wall is riddled with undercuts and overhangs. To the north of the driveway, a peninsula buttresses out. A large barrel sponge is perched atop a promontory at 90ft, making for a nice wide-angle shot. The wall is liberally decorated with colorful tube and stove-pipe sponges, wire corals and an occasional black coral tree.

Divers often see reef sharks and turtles in this area. Eagle rays also cruise by on occasion.

Pairs of butterflyfish ply Driveway's shallow waters.

18 Brandywine (Brandy-Glass Sponge)

This flat fringing reef is covered with closely packed coral heads. The wall begins between 45 and 50ft and is a sheer drop in most areas. In one section of the wall, the coral buttress extends outward and forms a steep slope.

You'll find large barrel sponges all along the wall. Brandywine is named after a 6ft-tall barrel sponge, shaped like a brandy snifter, that adorns the sloping buttress reef at about 80ft. This sponge is large enough to fit a couple of small divers inside, but don't touch it—it is a couple hundred years old.

Along the lip of the wall, divers will encounter large green moray eels amid the coral heads. Hawksbill and loggerhead turtles are seen here on a regular basis. Gobies and Pederson shrimp frequent the area's numerous cleaning stations.

Location: West wall

Depth Range: 30-90ft+ (9-27m+)

Access: Boat or live-aboard

Expertise Rating: Novice

The back reef has an isolated scattering of coral heads measuring 6 to 10ft across. Some of these are high-profile coral heads, towering 10ft or more above the sand bottom. The corals in the shallows include common sea fans, angular sea whips, venus sea fans and wide-mesh sea fans. Nurse sharks cruise through the shallows here quite regularly. The shallow sandy areas are also a good place to look for flying gurnard.

Be Gentle with the Giant

Giant barrel sponges are normally found at depths below 40ft (12m). The largest specimens typically occur in deep water along the forward slope of a reef. However, in the Turks and Caicos they are frequently found on the flat reef surfaces on top of the walls or on the back reefs. They can grow to more than 6ft (2m) high with an equal diameter.

Divers are often tempted to sit on or in these large sponges. Barrel sponges grow only 1 inch (2cm) per year—a sponge as large as a diver may be more than 100 years old. Touching or handling the barrel sponges is discouraged because the lip breaks easily, disrupting the organism's flow of water and food. Breakage also allows the entry of organisms that can weaken or even kill the sponge.

Growing only 1 inch per year, a large barrel sponge may be more than 100 years old.

19 | White Face (The Anchor)

White Face is along the southern end of the West Caicos wall, just outside of West Caicos Marine National Park. The steep white cliffs that are the site's namesake are clearly visible above the nearby shoreline. These cliffs are only 10 to 12ft high.

Location: West wall

Depth Range: 40-90ft+ (12-27m+)

Access: Boat or live-aboard

Expertise Rating: Novice

The top of the wall here is approximately 50ft deep. The coral is lush and varied. A gully slices down through the top of the reef, opening out on the wall at about 85ft. As you make your way through the gully, you will find an old encrusted anchor dating back to the 1600s. The anchor, which is partly overgrown with encrusting corals, is wedged against the north side of the gully. Viewed from the ocean side the anchor is clearly visible, but it blends in with the corals from the other direction and can be easily overlooked.

The undercuts on both sides of the gully's sandy bottom are filled with life. As you swim through, you may encounter curious black jacks, groupers and angelfish. A resident Caribbean reef shark likes to cruise through the gully—it is not shy about getting close to divers. A large anemone sits just outside the gully on the north side.

The wall in this area is a sheer vertical drop adorned with large barrel, rope and tube sponges. Continue your dive to the

An encrusted anchor adorns the cut at White Face.

north and follow the drop-off. Be on the lookout for pelagics, including eagle rays, reef sharks and turtles.

Swim back along the top of the wall, where schools of goatfish, grunts and snappers are common. The abundant corals along the back reef teem with life.

If you have plenty of air left or want an interesting shallow dive (between 5 and 10ft), head up toward the shoreline. Nurse sharks are fairly common there and lemon sharks make regular appearances.

This site also makes a great night dive, when you can count on seeing at least one nurse shark and a couple of Caribbean reef sharks cruising around under your boat.

Lemon sharks are often seen along the ironshore at White Face.

20 Sunday Service

Sunday Service is at the very end of the West Caicos wall. The fringe reef at the top of the wall varies greatly in width and is mostly a thin layer of coral with small coral heads. The fringe reef tops out at 45 to 50ft and slopes steeply to the edge of the wall at 65ft. One main and several smaller sand chutes cut through the top of the fringe reef.

Location: West wall

Depth Range: 15-80ft+ (5-24m+)

Access: Boat or live-aboard

Expertise Rating: Novice

This part of the West Caicos wall has eroded, so it slopes in most places, especially on the fringing reef. The wall itself is covered primarily with sea rods, sea plumes and a variety of hard corals, such as plate, star and brain corals. Divers frequently see reef sharks between high tide and two to three hours after high tide, when the tidal flow carries nutrients out of the shallows. The smaller fish are out feeding then, which attracts the larger predators.

The back reef is like a jigsaw puzzle of low-profile strip reefs. Giant sea rods, sea whips and sea plumes in shades of tan, purple and lavender grow in the sand between these reefs. At the north end of this site, just north of the mooring, a massive pillar coral stands more than 7ft tall.

As you swim into the shallows, the hardpan steeply slopes up from 25ft to about 15ft. Continue swimming toward the ironshore until you get to the mini-wall at the shoreline. Make your way along this mini-wall, swimming in and out of the small cove areas. Corals here include healthy stands of elkhorn corals, pink and lavender common sea fans and wide mesh sea fans. This site seems to have quite a few of the rare fingerprint cyphomas. Fingerprint cyphomas and flamingo tongues feed exclusively on soft corals, primarily sea fans and sea rods, so look for them near their food sources.

Deep gullies run perpendicular to the shoreline. One of these gullies dead-ends in a small cove with an underwater arch that is large enough to swim through. It is common to see large nurse sharks in this area, as well as small lemon sharks. A bull shark will occasionally cruise around the southern tip of the island and make a cameo appearance. Also be on the lookout for loggerhead turtles in this area.

Be on the lookout for loggerhead turtles in this area.

French Cay Dive Sites

French Cay is an uninhabited sandy cay on the southwest side of the Caicos Bank, 15 miles (24km) southeast of West Caicos and 16 miles (26km) south of Providenciales. Live-aboard boats frequently access this remote area, and day boats from Providenciales occasionally make the 60- to 90-minute run.

The cay is surrounded by a maze of coral heads and stands of elkhorn coral, interspersed with sand patches. Spotted eagle rays are commonly seen here in 5 to 10ft (2 to 3m) of water. Snorkelers will find many places to explore in the shallows around French Cay.

A white-sand beach surrounds the islet. Much of the beach is piled high with empty conch shells. The interior of the cay, which is covered with low vegetation,

Elkhorn corals decorate the shallows around French Cay.

is a wildlife refuge (French Cay Sanctuary) used by terns during nesting season. Visitors must have permission to visit the island and should stay away from the nesting areas in the center of the island.

During the summer months the shallow areas around the cay are breeding grounds for nurse sharks. Visitors should always use caution around nurse sharks, especially during the mating season (when they are most likely to become agitated). Nurse sharks are wild animals and can be dangerous if provoked.

Several excellent dive sites lie to the south and southwest of French Cay. Another excellent site, the west side of West Sand Spit, is just a few miles southeast of the cay.

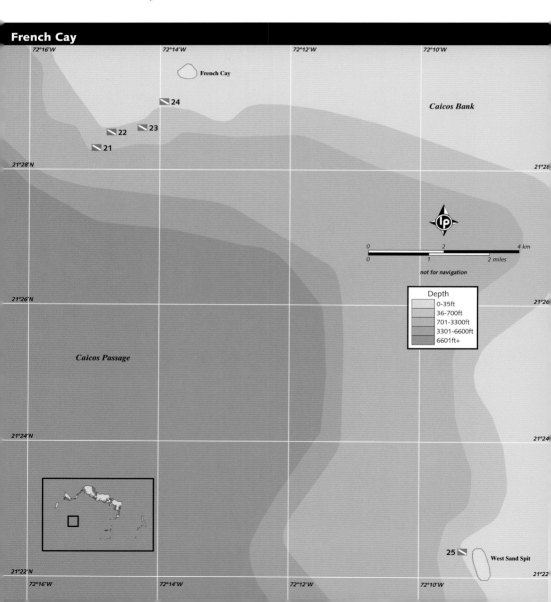

French Cay

French Cay Dive Sites

		Good Snorkeling	Novice	Intermediate	Advanced
21	Double D			●	
22	Rock 'n' Roll			●	
23	The G-Spot			●	
24	Half-Mile Reef			●	
25	West Sand Spit			●	

21 Double D

At this site along the wall that lies west-southwest of French Cay, Double D means double the excitement because of the abundance of big animals—sharks, hawksbill turtles and eagle rays are always around. It is also a good place to take wide-angle photos of elephant ear sponges and deepwater sea fans or portraits of pelagics.

A ridge at 50ft parallels the drop-off. This ridge slopes down to the top of the wall, which plummets vertically from

Location: 2 miles (3km) WSW of French Cay

Depth Range: 40-110ft+ (12-34m+)

Access: Boat or live-aboard

Expertise Rating: Intermediate

about 90ft to more than 6,000ft. The top of the reef has a solid covering of

Hawksbill turtles hang out near Double D's mooring.

hard corals, soft corals and sponges. A medium-sized hawksbill turtle, totally unafraid of divers, is often seen cruising along the edge of the drop-off.

The mooring is atop the larger of two coral mounds that sit just inshore of the wall. If you look beneath the coral mound's overhangs, you may discover snoozing hawksbill turtles. Large spotted scorpionfish often hang out here. One may allow divers to get a close peek at its rather grizzled countenance. However, be wary of its venomous spines, which are capable of causing a great deal of pain.

If you begin the dive at the mooring and continue over the wall, you will come upon a huge deepwater gorgonian at about 110ft, adjacent to a good-sized elephant ear sponge. About 25ft farther along the reef at 100ft is an even larger elephant ear sponge angled slightly upward. You'll see many deep-water gorgonians as you descend along the wall.

Many large, bright orange elephant ear sponges grow on top of the wall in depths shallower than 60ft. Schools of fish frequent this area, especially when the tide is sweeping nutrients from the shallows. Atlantic spadefish, horse-eye jacks, barracuda, bar jacks, turtles, eagle rays and several large reef sharks are frequently encountered as well.

22 Rock 'n' Roll

Rock 'n' Roll is obviously named for the rough conditions frequently encountered at French Cay. A boat at anchor here will often "rock and roll" in the heavy currents and generally turbulent conditions. When the ocean is rough, dive boats have

Location: 1 mile (2km) WSW of French Cay

Depth Range: 25-80ft+ (8-24m+)

Access: Boat or live-aboard

Expertise Rating: Intermediate

Long-horn nudibranchs come out at night to forage for food.

nowhere to hide (there is no protected anchorage). It is not advisable to dive here unless the conditions are calm.

The steep wall, oriented roughly east to west, has slight indentations. It begins at about 65ft and plummets vertically into the abyss. Just inside the lip of the drop-off, a steeply sloping strip of fringe reef sits between 50 and 65ft.

The top of the wall is incredibly lush. Overgrown low-profile spur-and-groove formations run perpendicular to the wall. The marine life is monochromatic— mostly shades of brown. However, you'll find many large barrel sponges, brown tube sponges and soft corals.

The mooring, in approximately 45ft, is not far from a sand patch. A school of squirrelfish almost always hangs out amid the staghorn corals that grow to one side of this sand patch. A wide diversity and abundance of tropical fish inhabit this area. Commonly seen marine life includes hawksbill turtles, eagle rays, Caribbean reef sharks, stoplight parrotfish, schools of jacks and Atlantic spadefish.

A tour through the mooring area and the shallower parts of this site makes for an excellent night dive. After sunset, divers will often encounter Atlantic squid, pygmy squid, nurse sharks and Caribbean reef

sharks, lobster, spotted and green moray eels and long-horn nudibranchs out in the open on the reef.

The best time to dive this site is on an incoming tide through a bit past high tide, when visibility is best. When the visibility is good, the barrel sponges and schools of spadefish make for excellent wide-angle photo subjects.

Divers see reef squid on most night dives at French Cay.

23 The G-Spot

G-Spot is an exciting dive, so-named (reportedly) because "it's so hard to find, but well worth it when you do." The top of the wall is at 40 to 50ft, with a sheer vertical drop-off to 6,000ft. The wall is covered with an assortment of soft coral, as well as deepwater gorgonians. The top of the wall offers many stands of pillar corals, large barrel sponges and low-profile coral ridges.

Adjacent to the mooring is one of the best walls in the Turks and Caicos. The top of the wall turns at a 90° angle. The section of the drop-off on the south side of the turn (to the right as you face the sea) is covered with beautiful deepwater

Location: 1 mile (2km) WSW of French Cay

Depth Range: 40-80ft+ (12-24m+)

Access: Boat or live-aboard

Expertise Rating: Intermediate

gorgonians from the top of the wall at 50ft down into the depths. Divers will find elephant ear sponges, barrel sponges and colorful tube sponges amid these gorgonians. When the visibility clears on an incoming tide, this wall is awesome.

During tidal changes, a lot of activity happens near the point. Schooling fish love this area, especially when the tide is sweeping nutrients from the shallows. Jacks, barracuda and other pelagics, including eagle rays, are frequently encountered as well. Even humpback whales are occasionally seen off the wall from January to March. Caribbean reef sharks are always present at this site, day and night.

G-Spot is also an incredible night dive. Use your dive light to reveal the wall's really intense nighttime colors. Drop over the lip of the wall and look amid the sea fans for basket stars with outstretched arms. Divers will often see bristle worms, which can measure up to 12 inches long and more than an inch wide, climbing out on the sea fans. You can literally fill your camera's framer with larger-than-life macro images of these critters' faces.

While you swim back through the shallows to the boat, horse-eye jacks and black jacks will dart in and out of your light in pursuit of baitfish schools. If you hang out beneath the dive boat, you will see Caribbean reef sharks patrolling the top of the reef, casually swimming in and out of view in un-predictable patterns. The resident Caribbean reef sharks are not at all shy about approaching divers, often coming within arm's reach. Some sharks habitually cruise back and forth 10 to 15ft beneath the boat.

The photo and video opportunities are so

G-Spot is literally covered with corals and sponges.

numerous that it's hard to choose between them. On the one hand this site offers an incredible wall dive, and on the other hand you can see sharks up close and personal. If you want it all in one dive, drop over the wall to 70 or 80ft at the beginning of the dive to capture the incredible beauty of the wall, then hang out at 40ft under the boat to visit with the resident reef sharks.

Close Encounters

Many divers seek out close encounters with sharks. When divemasters tell you to be prepared for such an encounter, heed their word—it might make for a very rewarding dive. Here is the author's account of one such circumstance:

"I was standing on the dive platform of the *Aggressor* live-aboard, moored at G-Spot. As I prepared to enter the water, the divemaster remarked that the last time he jumped in here, he was buzzed by a shark right under the boat. I quickly fiddled with the controls of my camera, pre-setting aperture and f-stop for a close encounter...ya' just never know. I jumped in, descended to about 10ft (3m) and started kicking slowly toward the bow, just under the keel of the boat. Visibility was about 80ft (24m).

"As if on cue, a large, bulky Caribbean reef shark swam toward me from the direction of the mooring line. I froze, trying to imitate a piece of plankton, and carefully adjusted my camera's manual focus lever as the 7-footer kept getting larger in the viewfinder. I expected him to veer off, and I waited patiently for him to start to turn. I waited...and waited...holding my breath.

"I suddenly realized that the shark's nose was just inches from my wide-angle lens. I depressed the shutter...and heard my camera make that sound that indicates the film was loading properly. It also told me that the camera had not taken a shot. The shark cruised on by and disappeared behind me. I had a brief discussion with myself and chalked it up to another one of those missed opportunities.

"I glanced back and watched as the shark slowly made a wide circle, coming around for another pass. This interaction continued for about half an hour, with the shark cruising out of sight and then back under the boat.

"Several days later on another trip to French Cay, the boat was anchored at Rock 'n' Roll. My buddy and I asked to be dropped off at G-Spot to take some pictures of the wall. After shooting most of my roll, we ascended to 15ft (5m) to make the long swim back to the boat. First one shark and then two more rose from the top of the plateau and began circling us. No fins down, no aggressive passes, just a continuous circling only 20ft (6m) away. When we swam beneath the keel of the boat, only a few feet from the surface, one of the sharks cruised up to us through a school of horse-eye jacks. This was pretty brazen, even for a shark. When I trade emails with the captain of the boat, he usually remarks, '*Your* crazy sharks are back.'"

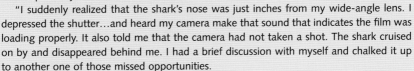

24 Half-Mile Reef

You can explore three different areas at Half-Mile Reef—the lush back reef, the vertical wall and a mini-wall that lies between the two. The mini-wall, which drops from 35 to 50ft, is overgrown with large sponges, sea rods and sea whips. The larger wall begins at 50ft and drops to extreme depths. Many large, red deep-water sea fans cling to this deeper wall.

Location: S end of French Cay

Depth Range: 25-80ft+ (8-24m+)

Access: Boat or live-aboard

Expertise Rating: Intermediate

The permanent mooring, on the back reef, is in 35ft of water. This area is dotted with large soft corals (sea fans, whips and plumes), as well as sponges that protrude from small mounds of hard corals. Schools of horse-eye jacks and Atlantic spadefish frequent this area.

Among the many pelagics on the back reef and on the wall are turtles, rays and sharks. Divers will also encounter large lobsters and pairs of beautiful tropicals, including white-spotted filefish, scrawled filefish, butterflyfish and large angelfish.

When you dive here just before high tide, concentrate on wide-angle photos of divers with deepwater gorgonians and large sponges. Use the wide-angle setting on your camcorder as well, to capture divers swimming off the wall and amid the large corals and sponges on top of the wall.

Atlantic spadefish and horse-eye jacks school above Half-Mile Reef.

25 West Sand Spit

This dive site, southeast of French Cay along the west edge of the Caicos Bank, is visited infrequently. It has absolutely no protection from rough seas. The currents can be quite strong here, and the site can be dived only when conditions are extremely calm. Even live-aboard dive boats out of Provo can dive here only two or three times a year. Rough seas, strong currents and the possibility of getting into extreme depths can turn this into an advanced dive site.

The site's namesake, a long sand spit that runs north to south, breaks the surface at low tide. At high tide West Sand Spit is completely covered with water. The visibility is variable, dependant upon the tidal flow. On the outgoing tide (when high tide changes to low tide) a great deal of sediment and silt is carried from the shallows of the bank, reducing visibility to 60ft or less. On the incoming tide, visibility often dramatically improves, especially when clean water from the open ocean is brought in during the two hours before high tide.

The wall, which slopes off fairly steeply from about 50ft, forms a semicircular shape on the west side of the spit. The northwest edge of this wall is particularly lush, with a variety of large, healthy sponges and corals. Incredible numbers of netted barrel sponges, giant barrel sponges, brown and yellow tube sponges, lavender rope sponges and leathery barrel sponges grow along the wall's face. Divers will also find small, bright orange elephant ear sponges scattered about. Giant sea rods and other soft corals have sprouted up all over the reef, and you'll even find a few large pillar corals in the shallower areas.

Location: 10 miles (16km) SE of French Cay

Depth Range: 40-100ft+ (12-30m+)

Access: Boat or live-aboard

Expertise Rating: Intermediate

The gently sloping terrain on top of the wall sports a variety of hardy filter feeders. Magnificent stands of pillar corals, large barrel sponges, large sea whips and sea rods rise up from the bottom.

A mini-wall drops vertically to a gently sloping sandy bottom at 100 to 120ft, which in turn drops off again to incredible depths.

In September and October divers will frequently encounter squadrons of eagle rays swimming along the mini-wall and on top of the wall. Year-round, divers will see large southern stingrays, octopuses, barracuda, pairs of whitespotted filefish, an assortment of jacks and hawksbill turtles. Nurse sharks and Caribbean reef sharks are encountered on most dives.

Approach filefish with slow movements.

South Caicos Dive Sites

South Caicos is on the southeastern edge of the Caicos Bank and along the western edge of the Turks Island Passage, 22 miles (35km) west of Grand Turk. The main tourism center is East Harbour, formerly called Cockburn Harbour, on the southwest coast. At one time this island was a major salt producing area. Today, queen conch and spiny lobster are the primary exports, and it's a major sport-fishing destination.

Where the Caicos Bank borders the Turks Island Passage, depths can abruptly plunge from 20ft (6m) to 7,000ft (2,100m). Despite this, the island offers beautiful shallow coral gardens appropriate even for novice divers. The best diving is along the edge of the Caicos Bank on the south end of the island, from the southeast point of South Caicos westward along the southeast shore of Long Cay. The sites near East Harbour are protected from the prevailing tradewinds.

This is one of the best areas in the Turks and Caicos for fish life, with lots of eagle rays, sharks, turtles and jacks. In the summer, divers will frequently see schools of eagle rays that sometimes number 100 to 150 animals.

Though South Caicos has only one dive operation at this time, live-aboards visit the area, as do occasional day boats out of Grand Turk when conditions are extremely calm. The dive sites are all within the boundaries of the Admiral Cockburn Land and Sea National Park. Two sites close to East Harbour are frequently visited by dive operators: Airplane Wreck and The Arch.

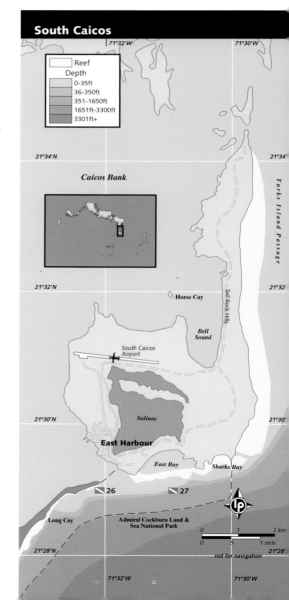

South Caicos

Reef
Depth
0-35ft
36-350ft
351-1650ft
1651ft-3300ft
3301ft+

Caicos Bank

Turks Island Passage

Horse Cay

Sail Rock Hills

Bell Sound

South Caicos Airport

Salinas

East Harbour

East Bay

Sharks Bay

26

27

Long Cay

Admiral Cockburn Land & Sea National Park

0   1   2 km
0   .5   1 mile

not for navigation

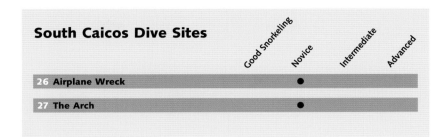

South Caicos Dive Sites

	Good Snorkeling	Novice	Intermediate	Advanced
26 Airplane Wreck		●		
27 The Arch		●		

26 | Airplane Wreck

This wreck dive is in the Admiral Cockburn Land and Sea National Park, inshore of the wall, at the southeast end of Long Cay. The mooring is in 35ft of water, on the shore side of the wreck.

In the 1970s, Turk-Cai Watersports stripped the engines and other equipment from the wreck of a Convair 440 airplane and sank it in 40ft of water near the harbor entrance. Since then, storms have battered and partially broken up the plane, but it's still somewhat intact.

Location: SE end of Long Cay

Depth Range: 10-50ft (3-15m)

Access: Boat or live-aboard

Expertise Rating: Novice

The wreck now sits in 45 to 50ft of water on a relatively flat sand-and-rubble bottom. The cockpit and the tail have broken off. One wing is still attached to the fuselage and divers can swim underneath that wing and through the cabin. The other wing has broken off, but lies in place at the side of the plane. Many gorgonians grow on the top of the fuselage. Small schools of grunts and snappers frequently take refuge inside the wreck.

Gray angelfish often approach divers quite closely.

The back reef adjacent to the wreck is characterized by high-profile spur-and-groove formations that run perpendicular to the wall. A mini-wall in the hardpan rises from 25ft to less than 10ft on the shore side of the plane. In the shallows above this mini-wall you'll find a scattering of sea fans, sea rods and fire coral.

The wall is a sheer drop from 60 to 110ft, where it plateaus briefly and then drops into the abyss. Common residents include Spanish hogfish, lizardfish, turtles, angelfish, tiger groupers, horse-eye jacks and moray eels. Eagle rays frequently cruise by, while octopuses, giant crabs and spotted morays make appearances on night dives.

PIERS VAN DER WALT

Schoolmasters seek shelter within Airplane Wreck.

27 The Arch

The Arch's namesake—a 15ft-wide natural coral arch that spans 25ft and stands 6ft tall—stretches between two parallel gullies in this site's back reef. The bottom of the arch is approximately 45ft deep.

Though the arch is not instantly apparent, you can find it fairly easily. The back reef gently slopes down from an elkhorn fringe reef that breaks the

Location: S end of South Caicos, E of the cut to the harbor entrance

Depth Range: 30-90ft (9-27m)

Access: Boat or live-aboard

Expertise Rating: Novice

surface. At 30 or 35ft you'll see a shallow sand pit approximately 40ft across. An opening out of this sand pit leads to a channel. The arch connects this channel with another parallel channel. Both run perpendicular to the drop-off. Their sides are 5 or 6ft high.

A large loggerhead turtle hangs out in the second channel, occasionally resting in a depression opposite the base of the arch. Hawksbill turtles and nurse sharks also frequent this site.

A mini-wall drops from 60 or 75ft along the site's outside edge. The bottom slopes from the base of this mini-wall to the top of the main wall at about 85ft. In this sloping area divers will find huge southern stingrays foraging in the sand patches between the coral heads.

At the top of the deeper wall you'll find a 15- to 40ft-wide band of fringing coral. The wall is composed primarily of star and plate corals.

South Caicos boasts a lot of tropical fish. You'll see schools of margates, grunts and snappers, as well as horse-eye jacks, angelfish and filefish. The arch, which is occasionally inhabited by an assortment of large fish, makes a good frame for wide-angle photos and videos of divers swimming through it. Whether taking still or video images, have your dive buddy swim through the arch from the side opposite you so that you can get images of the critters under the archway between you and your buddy.

Be careful not to disturb the experiments being conducted by the "Field of Studies" program headquartered in South Caicos. PVC pots have been placed inside the archway to measure the coral growth rate.

At night, divers frequently see nurse sharks along the sandy bottom.

Grand Turk Dive Sites

Grand Turk is about 7 miles (11km) long and 1½ miles (2.5km) wide at its widest point. Though it is the capital and seat of government of the Turks and Caicos Islands, the pace here is a lot slower than that of Provo, where growth and development of upscale tourism is quite evident. The island has a number of small, quaint hotels on Front and Duke Streets, just a few footsteps from the beach. The island's three shore-based dive operations are also in this area.

The best diving in Grand Turk is along the wall, which is not far off the island's western shoreline. The lip of the wall is just 25 to 50ft (8 to 15m) deep. With the prevailing trade winds coming out of the southeast, these sites are protected throughout most of the year. The sites on the northern and southern ends of the wall sometimes experience a bit more current and decreased visibility due to tidal changes, especially during outgoing tides.

Many of the reefs have moorings—new ones are added and old ones are replaced on a regular basis. All of the sites on the west wall lie within the protected

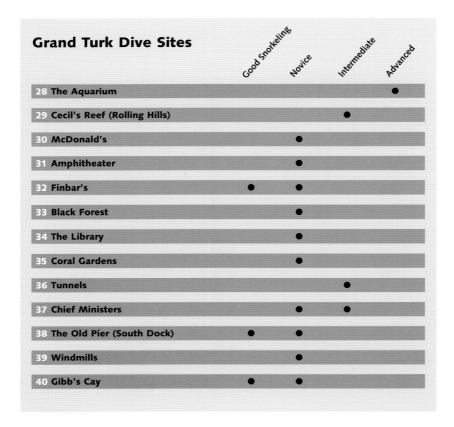

Grand Turk Dive Sites	Good Snorkeling	Novice	Intermediate	Advanced
28 The Aquarium				●
29 Cecil's Reef (Rolling Hills)			●	
30 McDonald's		●		
31 Amphitheater		●		
32 Finbar's	●	●		
33 Black Forest		●		
34 The Library		●		
35 Coral Gardens		●		
36 Tunnels			●	
37 Chief Ministers		●	●	
38 The Old Pier (South Dock)	●	●		
39 Windmills		●		
40 Gibb's Cay	●	●		

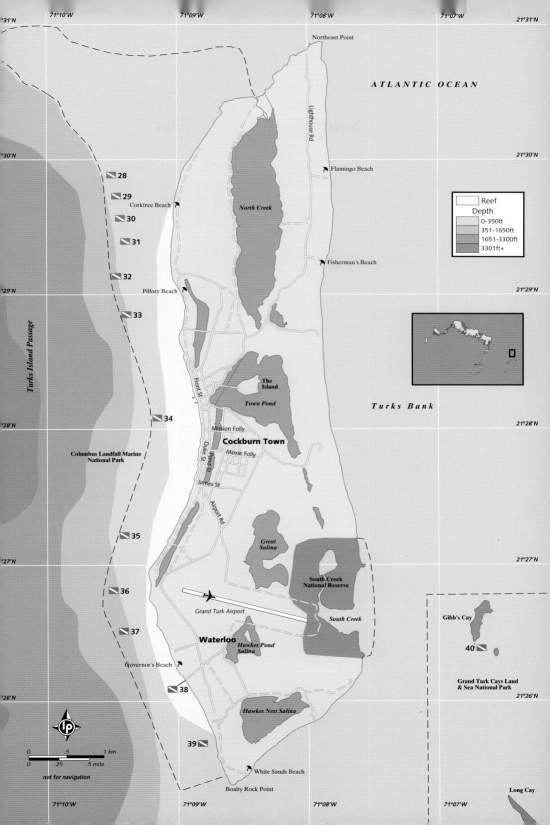

area of Columbus Landfall Marine National Park. Most of the sites are boat dives and are just a few minutes' trip from shore. The day-boat operators usually pick up divers from the beach south of Cockburn Town (near the dive stores) or near various waterfront hotel properties. Boats are typically small, which keeps the dive groups small and makes it easy to load gear from the beach. Bimini awnings provide divers with shade.

In addition to the sites along Grand Turk's wall, divers should visit the Old Pier/South Dock area, which is a shore dive with incredible macro marine life. A snorkel and barbecue trip to Gibb's Cay (just east of Grand Turk) to swim with the southern stingrays is also a must.

28 The Aquarium

The Aquarium is so named because of the incredible number and variety of fish that you'll find here. It's a spectacular deep dive at the northernmost end of Grand Turk's western wall, where the wall transforms from a sheer vertical drop to a series of ridges and sand valleys. Much of this site is an exaggerated, oversized spur-and-groove formation.

Location: W side of Grand Turk

Depth Range: 50-130ft+ (15-40m+)

Access: Boat or live-aboard

Expertise Rating: Advanced

The mooring is at 55ft atop a massive coral ridge that runs perpendicular to the edge of the wall. A sand channel runs along either side of this ridge. If you follow the channels away from the wall, they open onto a large, flat, sandy horseshoe-shaped area between 60 and 65ft deep. In this area, divers often see flying gurnard, flounder and southern stingrays shadowed by small jacks.

If you follow the sand channel on the south side of the ridge toward the wall,

Grunts and schoolmasters congregate in canyons at the south end of The Aquarium.

Deepwater sea fans line the steeply terraced foreslope at The Aquarium.

it opens up into a wide sandy bowl that slopes to 140ft. Divers often encounter large schools of fish in the bowl, including ocean triggerfish, schoolmasters, horse-eye and crevalle jacks, blue runners, yellowtail snappers and barracuda.

As you progress southward, you'll pass a series of large, parallel ridges divided by sand or hardpan channels that run perpendicular to the wall. On the inshore side, the tops of these ridges rise to 40ft. Several tall stands of healthy pillar coral grow atop the ridges. Toward the wall the ridges terrace steeply seaward. This area is covered with large deepwater gorgonians and tall sea rods. Wide-angle images of divers above the sea fans make for dramatic photos.

At the southern end of this dive site, a huge box canyon extends up into the back reef and dead-ends. The steep hard coral sides rise to 35ft. At the end of the canyon, large schools of snappers flow over the reef.

On the inshore side of the reef, divers will find garden eels and stingrays on the sandy bottom, parrotfish, and sometimes hawksbill turtles foraging for food. On the wall and in the bowl look for a wide variety of invertebrates, including orange ball corallimorpharians, nudibranchs, tunicates and tube worms, as well as moray eels and octopuses.

Divers will occasionally see humpback whales migrating through this area in the winter months, but because of this site's exposed location on the northern end of Grand Turk, it's more likely to be adversely affected by winter storms. It is not always accessible between December and March.

This region's currents are usually slight to moderate and are largely dependent on the tides, but are also affected by weather. On outgoing tides, the water sweeps silt and sediment off the shallows at the north end of Grand Turk, drastically reducing visibility. When currents are strong, divers should limit their explorations to the bowl area and stay in the lee of the ridges. Because of the possibility of strong currents and the extreme depths, this is generally considered an advanced dive.

29 Cecil's Reef (Rolling Hills)

Cecil's Reef is a very dramatic vertical wall at the north end of the Grand Turk wall. Divers can explore two vertical chimneys,

Location: W side of Grand Turk

Depth Range: 30-105ft+ (9-32m+)

Access: Boat or live-aboard

Expertise Rating: Intermediate

Elephant ear and tube sponges add a splash of color to Cecil's Reef.

one on the north end and one on the south end of the site. Begin the dive at the sand chute at the north end, swim over the lip of the wall and enter the chimney at 60ft. The chimney exits the wall at 105ft. The wall is adorned with small elephant ear sponges, sea rods, spindly gorgonians and tube sponges.

Continue to the lush back reef between 30 and 40ft, where you can finish your dive amid an assortment of soft corals and common sea fans. Tropical fish life includes a variety of grunts, durgons, parrotfish, trumpetfish and hamlets. Hawksbill turtles are frequent visitors.

Visibility varies widely with changes in the tides.

30 McDonald's

McDonald's is named after a large arched coral formation. The permanent mooring is in 30ft of water, about 300 yards from the shoreline.

Location: W side of Grand Turk

Depth Range: 30-130ft+ (9-40m+)

Access: Boat or live-aboard

Expertise Rating: Novice

Swim along the sandy bottom from the mooring to the edge of the wall. The arch, at the south end of the dive site, forms an open gateway through the high-profile fringing reef to the drop-off. The arch is wide enough for two divers to swim through at the same time, side by side. The cracks and fissures in the coral on either side of the arch often hide large lobsters or eels. As you pass through the arch, the bottom opens up onto a sand chute that drops off steeply. On the north and south sides of this sand chute, a vertical wall predominantly made up of hard plate corals and star corals is lavishly adorned with colorful sponges.

If you turn to the north (right) and drop down to about 100ft, you will discover many undercuts, overhangs and ledges as you make your way along the face of the wall. Be sure to take your time exploring these areas. Divers occasionally see seahorses and even frogfish here between 50 and 75ft. Ask your divemasters about any recent sightings on the reef. These animals are very territorial and often remain in the same location for a long time, as long as they are not disturbed.

At 120ft, a large, healthy, bright orange elephant ear sponge reaches out from the wall. Schools of creole wrasses, grunts, horse-eye jacks and ocean triggerfish often cruise along the wall. In the summer months it's not unusual to see a manta ray feeding here.

You can ascend from the top of the wall to the shallows through several steeply sloping cuts. On the north side of one of these cuts, a beautiful azure vase sponge sits out on a ledge at about 70ft.

The high-profile fringing reef at the top of the drop-off is massive. In several places the fringing reef extends small peninsula-like arms into the back reef. There are also large areas of sandy bottom with a few scattered coral heads.

You'll see lots of varieties of tropical fish in this area, including queen triggerfish, angelfish, blue tangs, coneys, graysbys and large groupers. On the sand, look for southern stingrays and flounder. As you cruise back to the mooring, keep an eye out for dozing turtles, spotted morays and green morays, all of which are pretty common in this area.

Look for azure vase sponges on McDonald's cuts and ledges.

31 Amphitheater

This site is named for an area that roughly resembles an amphitheater. This large bowl with a sand bottom is surrounded by a semicircular coral ridge (a large indentation in the wall itself) shaped like a cove or box canyon. If you sit on the sand bottom in the middle of the bowl with your back to the open ocean, you can look up at the vertical wall, which wraps around you like the towering seats of an amphitheater. The inshore edge of the amphitheater, which is the lip of the ridge, is at about 30ft. The permanent mooring is on the back reef in about 30ft of water, about 300 yards offshore.

Many sand chutes cut through the fringing reef at the top of the wall. Over the edge of the wall divers will find black coral trees, deepwater sea fans, large purple tube sponges and other vibrantly colored sponges.

The wall is contoured with undercuts, ledges and overhangs. On the wall and in the amphitheater area live a wide variety of invertebrates, including orange ball corallimorpharians, nudibranchs, tunicates and tube worms, as well as

Location: W side of Grand Turk

Depth Range: 30-130ft+ (9-40m+)

Access: Boat or live-aboard

Expertise Rating: Novice

moray eels and octopuses. Divers often encounter nurse sharks, schools of barracuda and turtles.

The back reef is a mix of patch reefs and sandy bottom. On the inshore side of the fringe reef, divers will find garden eels, parrotfish and stingrays on the sandy bottom. Common reef fish include hogfish, clown wrasses, yellow goatfish, squirrelfish and angelfish. The site's variety of macro subjects includes tunicates, feather duster worms, sharknose gobies and shrimp.

Photographers should seek out wide-angle shots of divers inside the amphitheater and of divers posing with the large brown and purple tube sponges found on the wall.

Filefish hide amid Amphitheater's deepwater sea fans.

32 Finbar's

Finbar's is an excellent wall dive opposite a house that was owned by the ex-chief minister of the same name. The mooring is shallow (in 25ft of water) and is about 250 yards from the shoreline.

The well-developed, wide fringing reef at the top of the wall begins at about 35ft. A coral buttress covered with coral heads and rubble extends from the wall and slopes gradually to the top edge of a promontory at about 75ft. If you follow the vertical wall down from this point, you will find 4- to 5-foot black coral branches extending from the wall. North of the promontory is a 6ft purple tube sponge colony at 86ft. The wall on either side of the promontory is fairly steep and is composed mostly of plate and star corals.

Schools of grunts, goatfish and snappers hang out in gullies and pockets in the reef between 30 and 60ft. Clouds of blue chromis are everywhere. The northern end of the site is bordered by a wide sand chute that isolates a large coral mound in 80ft of water. This mound is covered with deepwater gorgonians, black corals and large sponges.

The lush back reef is scattered with coral heads, pillar corals, sea fans and low-profile strip reefs. A resident nurse shark often cruises around the mooring. Common tropical fish include queen triggerfish, orangespotted filefish, parrotfish, creole wrasses, squirrelfish, porgies, sand tilefish and many varieties of hamlets, barracuda and angelfish. Moray eels and stingrays are pretty common. Quite a number of cleaning stations are in this area, with gobies, shrimp and juvenile Spanish hogfish doing the grunt work.

Except for the extreme depths along the wall, this site is considered a novice

Location: W side of Grand Turk

Depth Range: 25-90ft+ (8-27m+)

Access: Boat or live-aboard

Expertise Rating: Novice

dive. The area gets only a little current. It's frequently used for checkout dives or as a first-day orientation dive site. Because this site is pretty shallow and lush in the back reef areas, it's also a good area for snorkeling or free-diving.

This site lends itself to many types of photography. It's an excellent area for photographing cleaning stations, small schools of fish, friendly orangespotted filefish and nurse sharks.

A parrotfish seeks shelter between large sponges on Finbar's wall.

Cleaning Stations

Observant divers will find a variety of symbiotic relationships throughout the marine world—associations in which two dissimilar organisms participate in a mutually beneficial relationship.

One of the most interesting relationships is found at cleaning stations, places where one animal (or symbiont) advertises its grooming services to potential clients with inviting, undulating movements. Often this is done near a coral head.

Various species of cleaners such as gobies, juvenile hogfish and shrimp are dedicated to caring for their customers, which may include

A grouper awaits the services of a cleaner goby.

fish of all sizes and species. The fish hover in line until their turn comes. When the cleaner attends to a waiting customer—perhaps a grouper, parrotfish or even moray eel—it may enter the customer's mouth to perform dental hygiene and even exit through the fish's gills. Although the customer could have an easy snack, it would never attempt to swallow the essential cleaner. The large fish benefit from the removal of parasites and dead tissue, while the cleaner fish are provided with a meal.

Divers will find that if they carefully approach a cleaning station, they can get closer to many fish than is normally possible and observe behavior seen nowhere else on the reef. If cleaners are not occupied with fish, they may even try to attend to a diver's hygiene.

33   Black Forest

This site, aptly named for the plentiful black corals on the wall, is offshore from the currently closed Guanahani Hotel at the northern end of Cockburn Town. The permanent mooring is close to the edge of the wall in 35ft. Though this can be a deep dive, it's appropriate for novice divers, as the area is well protected and calm. Visibility ranges from 80 to 150ft.

The back reef's scattered coral heads give way to low-profile strip reefs interspersed with sand-and-rubble channels leading toward the drop-off. The seabed

Location: Grand Turk wall, N end of Cockburn Town

Depth Range: 35-105ft+ (11-32m+)

Access: Boat or live-aboard

Expertise Rating: Novice

features assorted soft and hard corals along the sand-and-rubble bottom, where divers will find an interesting assortment of creatures. Razorfish dive into the sand bottom and disappear from view when divers approach. Hard corals in the shallows include huge rosette and plate corals, as well as some stands of pillar coral.

Beginning at about 40ft, the fringing reef slopes to the lip of the vertical wall at 50ft. If you drop over the edge at the south end of the site, you will find a large elephant ear sponge at a depth of 65ft.

Swim north along the wall to a large, dramatic undercut loaded with five different varieties of black coral, starting in depths of only 50ft. There are as many as 100 black coral trees. This undercut extends about 100 yards along the wall and is well sheltered from surge and falling silt, so the corals are exceptionally healthy. At the north end of the site, a small ledge sticks out from the reef at a depth of 105ft. Here sits a solitary black coral branch next to a large tube sponge.

This wall is also a great night dive for experienced divers. Divers will find masses of tubastrea (bright yellow nocturnal cup corals), nudibranchs, shrimp, octopuses, moray eels and orange ball corallimorpharians. Near the base of the vertical wall at 100ft you will find several large orange elephant ear sponges.

Divers should take a dive light even during the day because the depression is heavily shadowed until late afternoon. Your light will help you see into the many cracks and fissures, which hide lobsters, octopuses and moray eels. A light will reveal the true colors of the "black" corals—varied hues of red and orange. Beneath the undercut, a sand shelf at about 100ft extends away from the wall, which then plummets vertically into the depths.

This site offers a great selection of photo subjects—wide-angle silhouettes of black coral and divers against the surface, portrait shots of divers with marine life and tubastrea corals on night dives.

Masses of tubastrea cup corals grow beneath the overhang.

34 The Library

The Library is a shallow wall dive just off the main street of Cockburn Town, across from the old Grand Turk library. You'll find a wide, low-profile fringing reef at the top of the wall in just 18 to 20ft of water. Because the wall starts at such a shallow depth, novice divers can experience the thrill of diving a vertical wall without getting in over their heads. Current and surge are minimal except when high winds blow from the west, which is rare.

The top of the wall is somewhat nondescript during the day, and the back reef is mostly rubble and sand. However, this is one of Grand Turks' most popular night dives. At night divers will encounter lobsters, eels, nudibranchs, octopuses, crabs, shrimp and tubastrea coral (bright yellow nocturnal cup corals). Orange ball corallimorpharians are abundant here.

Several mounds of coral-incrusted ballast stones are reminders that for several hundred years this area was used

Location: Grand Turk wall, offshore from the library

Depth Range: 20-100ft (6-30m)

Access: Boat or live-aboard

Expertise Rating: Novice

as an anchorage for vessels carrying salt from the island.

Divers can explore many crevices and undercuts along the wall and discover quite a few bright orange elephant ear sponges on the sheer drop-off. This is an excellent location to see and photograph an incredible variety of invertebrates.

The wall itself drops to 100ft, where a flat ledge extends for quite a distance before again plummeting into the depths of the Turks Island Passage. In a few areas along the top of the wall, the fringing reef forms small hills of coral. Small

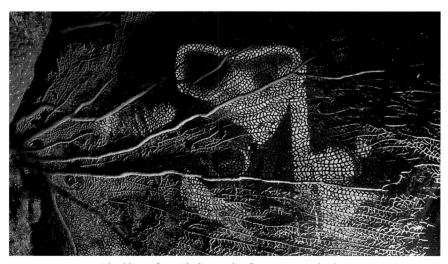

A backlit sea fan with diver makes for a unique night shot.

schools of cooperative grunts and snappers congregate in these areas, offering a good opportunity to get pictures of divers with fish. Divers will occasionally see schools of dolphins and manta rays in the summer.

During an incoming tide and for an hour or so after high tide, this area can be exceptionally clear. The combination of high ambient light in the shallows and clean water from the depths of the Turks Island Passage make this a great place for wide-angle photography, while the invertebrates and night life provide plenty of macro opportunities.

Corallimorpharians: The Anemones That Aren't

Orange ball corallimorpharians are said to be uncommon in the Caribbean, but are actually fairly common at The Library dive site in Grand Turk. Though they resemble (and are often mistaken for) anemones, corallimorpharians are not true anemones and are sometimes referred to as "false corals."

Orange balls are aptly named—they have a solitary polyp that consists of transparent tentacles tipped with bright orange balls. This animal is nocturnal and shuns light—if

you shine your light on one it will immediately begin to retract. Orange balls are 1 to 2 inches (2 to 5cm) across and have tentacles 1 to 2 inches (2.5 to 5cm) long. They are some of the most interesting and most attractive of the Caribbean's corallimorpharians. Divers should look for them on limestone substrate, in depths between 20 and 80ft (6 and 24m).

Corallimorpharians are often mistaken for anemones.

35 Coral Gardens

Coral Gardens is in the middle section of the Grand Turk wall. The permanent mooring, in 30ft of water, is about 250 yards offshore. The dive is basically made up of two separate levels. The first level, between 25 and 35ft, is a relatively flat back reef with scattered coral heads and a few low-profile reef ridges. The second level, between 65 and 90ft, is a lower plateau that extends out from the wall.

A mini-wall slopes steeply from the edge of the back reef to where the lower plateau begins. Spend the first part of the dive exploring the lower plateau, then ascend to the upper reef to explore the coral formations near the mooring.

On the plateau you'll find two sandy holes surrounded by plate corals, brain corals, sea fans, sea rods and large mounds of star corals together with small coral heads. This lower plateau slopes gently down to 90ft to the edge of another vertical wall, which drops to 7,000ft.

A lot of feeding activity takes place on the lower plateau. Divers should watch for groupers hunting schools of bar jacks,

Location: Grand Turk wall, S end of Cockburn Town

Depth Range: 25-90ft+ (8-27m+)

Access: Boat or live-aboard

Expertise Rating: Novice

as well as barracuda stalking schools of baitfish. Schools of snappers, grunts and medium-sized barracuda congregate at the top of the mini-wall. A number of large diver-friendly groupers cruise out in the open. Look for cleaning stations around the top of the mini-wall.

As you swim back to the boat, look for burrfish, smooth trunkfish and balloonfish. Green and hawksbill turtles often gather here in the spring. Schools of horse-eye jacks and small barracuda frequent the mooring area. Banded, spotfin and foureye butterflyfish pairs are also common and make for interesting photo opportunities.

36 Tunnels

This aptly named site features two natural tunnels on the face of the wall. The permanent mooring is at a depth of 35ft, 300 yards from the shoreline and about 10 yards from the lip of the drop-off.

A heavy coral buttress extends outward from the fringing reef at the top of the wall. A sandy back reef butts against this same high-profile fringing reef. Two sand chutes cut through the fringing reef to the drop-off, isolating a large section of the reef. The top of this massive, long coral island is at 40ft. The northern sand

Location: Grand Turk wall, W of airport

Depth Range: 35-60ft+ (11-18m+)

Access: Boat or live-aboard

Expertise Rating: Intermediate

chute is partially covered by a broken arch. The sides of the southern sand chute are covered with lush gorgonians and sponges.

A diver watches two smooth trunkfish along the back reef of Coral Gardens.

The entrance to the main tunnel is along the back side of this coral island, at a depth of about 50ft. This tunnel extends for about 25ft through the coral formation. It slopes gradually downward and emerges from the front of the reef at about 75ft. This tunnel is wide enough for only one diver at a time. Be careful not to stir up sediment from the bottom of the tunnel as you swim through.

If you turn to the left as you exit the tunnel, you will find a second tunnel. Though you can't swim through it, investigate the interior for a large grouper or swarming silversides.

At about 100ft, a plateau extends outward from the wall on the front side of the coral island. The area around the plateau is covered with a very large elephant ear sponge and an assortment of gorgonians, hard corals and colorful sponges. Divers encounter schools of horse-eye jacks, barracuda, blue chromis, creole wrasses, snappers and a variety of other jacks, as well as an occasional large grouper. In the summer, divers frequently see manta rays.

Though slight currents, overhead obstructions and the ever-present potential of extreme depths can be hazardous, most characterize this as an intermediate dive.

Manta rays are often seen during the summer at Tunnels.

37 Chief Ministers

Chief Ministers, sometimes referred to as "Ex-Chief Ministers," because of the precarious nature of the political position, is offshore of a former chief minister's house. This is a favorite Grand Turk site for fish photography.

The mooring is close to the edge of the wall, which drops off between 35 and 45ft. The fringe reef here is very lush, literally covered with soft corals and hard corals. This is the best place to take your fish portraits. The coral buttress that extends outward from the fringe reef is massive.

Location: Grand Turk wall, W of Governor's Beach

Depth Range: 35-80ft+ (11-24m+)

Access: Boat or live-aboard

Expertise Rating: Novice (back reef) Intermediate (chimney and wall)

Bluestriped grunts, schoolmasters and goatfish school near the mooring on top of the reef. These schools are tucked away next to the coral heads that rise up to 5ft above the surface of the fringe reef. These schooling fish are not at all skittish and allow divers to get very close.

The reef is also inhabited by an incredible assortment of tropicals, including scrawled filefish, angelfish, parrotfish, trumpetfish, groupers and butterflyfish. Invertebrates include social tube worms, flamingo tongues, Christmas tree worms and shrimp.

Approximately 150 to 200ft south of the mooring, a chimney is carved out of the wall. The chimney is fairly narrow, with an opening at 50ft, just below the lip of the reef, and an exit at 80ft on the wall.

You may see small hawksbill turtles cruising along the lush fringe reef at the top of the wall between the sandy areas and the drop-off.

The back reef is an expanse of powdery white sand dotted with garden eels. Southern stingrays lie buried in the sand during the day and forage on the sand flats at night.

Schoolmasters frequent the reeftop near the mooring at Chief Ministers.

38 The Old Pier (South Dock)

You have three different dive areas to choose from here: the newer commercial concrete pier, the old steel pier and an adjoining area to the north referred to as the pits. The commercial pier is used for loading and offloading of building materials, fuel, foodstuffs and other supplies for the island. The Peter Hughes live-aboard *Wind Dancer* uses the commercial dock for all of its departures. The *Turks and Caicos Aggressor* uses the commercial dock for its winter whale charters.

These three areas are typical "muck dives." They don't look that impressive

Location: SW end of Grand Turk

Depth Range: 10-25ft (3-8m)

Access: Boat or shore

Expertise Rating: Novice

when you first jump in, but a closer inspection reveals a treasure trove of interesting and unique marine life. This site is easily accessed from shore, but you may be able to talk a day-boat operator into anchoring nearby. If you are staying on one of the live-aboard vessles, you can end the trip with a dive or two in this area.

The commercial pier receives a great deal of boat activity at times, so be careful where you go. Ask a local operator for suggestions as to which areas around the pier are safe for diving. Normally the south side and the end of the pier have the least amount of traffic. Do not dive in an area where a ship is loading or offloading. Locals frequently fish off the pier, so keep away from fishing lines and watch out for tangles of discarded monofilament line.

The steel dock adjacent to the south dock was built in the mid-1960s to handle the island's shipping needs and to facilitate the construction of a U.S. missile tracking station used to track Mercury space launches. Boats that have

A black seahorse latches on to discarded fishing line.

docked here have used the area as a dump. Divers will find everything from beer cans, tires, broken pieces of cable and chain, boat fenders and concrete blocks to pieces of china and other tableware amid the rubble. Over the years, the sand and hardpan sea bottom north of the pier has been carved with ridges and pits by the churning of huge propellers from countless cargo ships.

Invariably, divers who visit this area are amazed at the incredible variety of miniature sea creatures here. For macrophotographers and videographers, this is an extremely productive area.

Look amid the pier's pilings, bits of rubble and debris to uncover a pair of spotted moray eels, several scorpionfish, golden shrimp (usually in pairs), a pygmy octopus, a batfish,

A tiny octopus emerges from a discarded clamshell.

flying gurnard and a host of other unusual animals. Most of these critters are proficient at camouflage, so they are often a bit hard to see. Several seahorses and frogfish have been seen at this site. A small black seahorse is a semipermanent resident and usually hangs out near the end of the pier. Frogfish often take on the texture and color of sponges, making them almost undetectable.

The surrounding sand flat is home to blue-spotted peacock flounder, large southern stingrays shadowed by bar jacks, and other creatures that live in the sand. Mantas have been seen around the pier and the adjacent beach areas during the summer months. The encrusted pilings and sides of the pier also offer colorful macrophotography subjects, such as nudibranchs and sponges.

39 Windmills

This site is named for the windmills that used to stand beside the salt lakes at the southern end of the island. A fringing reef, which tops out at 30 or 35ft, slopes steeply downward to approximately 75ft, where it plummets vertically into very deep water. The wall is adorned with large sea plumes, sea rods and other large soft corals. Off the wall, divers will frequently encounter turtles, eagle rays, porcupine-fish and ocean triggerfish. Several large gray angelfish and queen angelfish swim in and out of holes and recesses along the steep slope.

At the site's south end you'll find a short spur-and-groove formation. Its medium-profile ridges alternate with sand-and-rubble channels that run perpendicular to the drop-off. The back reef, which ranges from 20 to 30ft deep, is mostly composed of large coral heads on a sandy bottom. Healthy sea fans,

Location: SW end of Grand Turk

Depth Range: 30-90ft+ (9-27m+)

Access: Boat or live-aboard

Expertise Rating: Novice

black-ball sponges, bowl sponges and a variety of sea rods decorate the coral heads. The fish life on the back reef includes a large variety of parrotfish, angelfish, coneys, goatfish and other tropicals.

Divers are likely to see large southern stingrays and peacock flounder half-buried in the sand, as well as other common sand dwellers. The coral heads seem to have an unusually large number of interesting invertebrates, including large red-and-white rough fileclams and an interesting variety of shrimp, such as red snapping shrimp, Pederson cleaner shrimp, scarlet-striped cleaning shrimp, banded coral shrimp and squat anemone shrimp. Look closely at the sandy area for symbiotic pairings between Pederson shrimp and red snapping shrimp, which live together in holes also inhabited by corkscrew anemones. The north end of the site is marked by several massive submarine cables that run from the shallows out over the drop-off.

A diver takes a close look at a banded coral shrimp.

40 Gibb's Cay

A snorkel trip to Gibb's Cay, off the southeastern end of Grand Turk, is a must for all visitors to the island. Dive operators on Grand Turk make the trek to Gibb's Cay for a barbecue and a low-key snorkel encounter with the friendly southern stingrays of Sunray Beach.

This wide picturesque beach is bordered by protected, calm, shallow turquoise water. As soon as the boat approaches the beach, southern stingrays (which are often fed by visitors) are already winging their way into the shallows. As snorkelers step from their boat into the lapping surf, the stingrays will come up to greet them in water barely 6 inches deep. The stingrays will literally bump into swimmers and occasionally even climb atop snorkelers, making it easy for you to get wide-angle photos of stingrays and snorkelers together.

Location: SE of Grand Turk

Depth Range: 5-15ft (2-5m)

Access: Boat or shore

Expertise Rating: Novice

The stingrays are frequently joined by several other kinds of marine life, including barracuda, permits, large trunkfish, schooling baitfish and, occasionally, small lemon sharks.

The low bluffs above the beach are home to an osprey nest. Visitors may see these attractive birds flying around the beach. Black-headed sandpipers patrol the beach and wade in the shallows. An afternoon at Sunray Beach is an excellent way to unwind and enjoy sun, sand and sea.

Southern stingrays are not shy in the shallows at Gibb's Cay.

Salt Cay Dive Sites

Salt Cay is about 7 miles (11km) south of Grand Turk. The fairly flat, triangular cay is approximately 2½ sq miles (6.5 sq km). The highest point on the island is Taylor's Hill, which rises to about 60ft (18m) on the rocky eastern coast. Balfour Town, on the west shore, is the center of the island's tourism industry.

Humpback Whales

During the winter months, majestic humpback whales migrate from northern polar waters southward to the Silver Bank and the Mouchoir Bank (southeast of the Turks and Caicos Islands and north of the Dominican Republic). The Turks Island Passage, which separates the Turks Islands from the Caicos Islands, is part of their regular migratory route. Though seen throughout the Turks and Caicos in the winter, they are perhaps most common along the walls off Grand Turk, Salt Cay and South Caicos. The whales start to appear in late December and are present through most of March.

During the summer months the whales feed in the nutrient-rich polar waters. The humpback, a baleen whale, feeds on plankton and small fish. The baleen acts like an immense sieve, straining food from the water forced through the filterlike device. In the winter the whales come to the warm, shallow Caribbean waters to give birth and to mate. The calves are approximately 15ft (5m) long at birth and weigh about 1 to 1½ tons (900 to 1,350kg).

An average adult male humpback may reach 48ft (15m), while the females are usually a few feet longer. The weight of an adult humpback exceeds 35 tons (more than 30,000kg). The humpback has a stocky body and is readily recognizable by its long flippers, which can reach one-third of its overall length. The flipper of the Atlantic humpback is almost pure white on top and bottom.

Humpbacks are often seen breaching, blowing and tail slapping on the surface. Occasionally the whales are spotted from a boat near the dive sites and even underwater.

Over the years the whales seem to have become accustomed to divers and snorkelers. In the winter the *Wind Dancer* (Peter Hughes Diving) and the *Turks and Caicos Aggressor* liveaboards run trips to the Silver Bank to snorkel with humpback whales. The operators have found that mother humpbacks occasionally push their calves toward snorkelers and frequently hang motionless in the water for up to a half-hour while free-divers circle them for an up close look.

Only 60 or so people live on the island, which has a few outstanding dive operations and nice accommodations. Most dive sites range from five to ten minute's boat ride from Balfour Town, or about 45 minutes from Grand Turk.

One of the Turks and Caicos' most beautiful beaches stretches for 2 miles (3km) along the west half of Salt Cay's north shore. Point Pleasant, an excellent shallow snorkeling area near the northwest point, is accessible from shore and is the region's premier snorkeling site, with large conch, tarpon and spotted eagle rays. The wall off Salt Cay runs along the edge of the Turks Island Passage for the length of the island's western shoreline. Though several sites have permanent moorings, none are part of a protected park.

The *Endymion* wreck, one of the few diveable wrecks in Turks and Caicos, is a historical site that lies 10 miles (16km) south of Salt Cay.

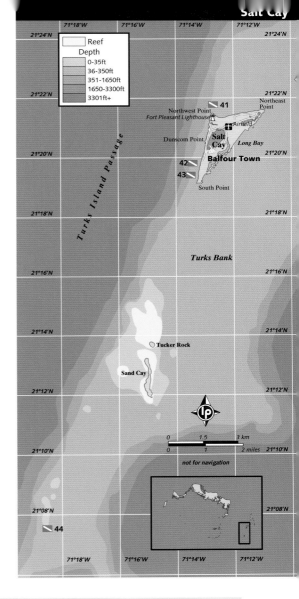

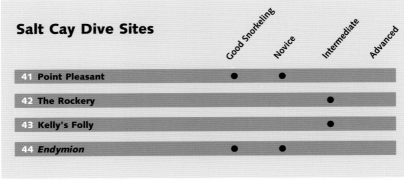

Salt Cay Dive Sites

	Good Snorkeling	Novice	Intermediate	Advanced
41 **Point Pleasant**	●	●		
42 **The Rockery**			●	
43 **Kelly's Folly**			●	
44 *Endymion*		●	●	

41 Point Pleasant

Point Pleasant is a shallow dive on the northwest end of Salt Cay, inshore of the wall. Spectacular stands of elkhorn and pillar corals rise to the surface. The currents and surge have carved caverns, swim-throughs and overhangs out of the corals and the limestone bottom.

Divers will often encounter one or more of the eagle rays that hang out in

Location: N of Northwest Point

Depth Range: Surface-25ft (8m)

Access: Boat or shore

Expertise Rating: Novice

this area. Tarpon, nurse sharks, French angelfish, southern stingrays, tiger groupers, schools of blue tangs and barracuda are also commonly seen here. African pompano and other large jacks make frequent appearances. This area offers some excellent opportunities for portraits of eagle rays, divers with pillar corals and elkhorn corals.

This is also one of the best snorkeling sites in the Turks and Caicos. Shallow water and bright sun combine for a shimmering display, with rays of light filtering down through the elkhorn corals. Snorkelers are able to get very close to large eagle rays, tarpon and an occasional turtle.

Point Pleasant sometimes gets a slight to moderate tidal current, but it's generally suitable for novice divers. Be aware of overhead obstructions and surge.

Spotted eagle rays frequent the shallows near Point Pleasant.

42 The Rockery

Huge deepwater gorgonians and black coral trees cling to this beautiful wall, which reaches up to 40ft. Though the wall drops to dizzying depths, its best features are found above 70ft. The visibility varies depending on tidal changes. Though it's not a hazardous or difficult site, surge may be moderate near the surface. This area offers some excellent wide-angle photographic opportunities for images of beautiful and colorful deepwater gorgonians.

Divers find large tiger groupers and Nassau groupers cruising along the wall and swimming in and out of crevices. Mantas visit in the summer months. Look for reef sharks and large jacks near the drop-off.

Location: Northwest Point

Depth Range: 30-70ft+ (9-21m+)

Access: Boat or live-aboard

Expertise Rating: Intermediate

The Rockery's back reef is covered with coral heads and sponges, including pillar corals, star corals, vase sponges, large elephant ear sponges and ivory tube sponges, as well as many sea plumes and sea rods. Nurse sharks are frequently encountered. Pairs of colorful butterflyfish are common, as are large queen triggerfish.

Tiger groupers swim in and out of The Rockery's crevices.

43 Kelly's Folly

The mooring at Kelly's Folly is on the back reef at 27ft. Stands of elkhorn coral grow in the shallows toward the shoreline. Low- to medium-profile strip-reef ridges, alternating with sand channels, run perpendicular to the wall atop the reef and gradually slope to about 40ft. Here you'll find many stands of pillar corals between 1 and 5ft high.

The slope drops steeply from 40ft to the top of the vertical wall at 80 or 90ft. Sea fans, plumes and rods cover the plate and star corals. The wall is adorned with black coral branches and elephant ear sponges.

Marine life is abundant and varied at this site, with schools of blue tangs constantly moving from place to place around the reef. Grunts, goatfish and snappers school around the soft corals.

Location: W of South Point

Depth Range: 25-80ft (8-24m)

Access: Boat or live-aboard

Expertise Rating: Intermediate

This area's tropical fish typically include queen triggerfish, pufferfish, parrotfish, hog snappers, butterflyfish, groupers, spotted drums and queen angelfish. Turtles are also frequently seen cruising the top of the reef slope.

The visibility varies depending on tidal changes. A great deal of silt and plankton can be swept off the Turks Bank on an outgoing tide.

Pillar corals rise from the shallow seafloor at Kelly's Folly.

44 *Endymion*

The HMS *Endymion* is an unsalvaged 18th-century British warship. The relentless pounding of the ocean has broken up the wreck, whose remains lie scattered in 30 to 40ft of water. Lying exposed on the bottom are 18 cannons and nine large anchors. Nearby lie the remains of two other ships—a Civil War steamer and an unidentified ship dating to around 1900. Because of the shallow depths and bright ambient light, the remains of the wrecks and the surrounding marine life are great photo subjects.

Lots of large fish inhabit the area, which is filled with healthy sponges and corals, including elkhorn, staghorn and pillar corals, as well as a variety of sea fans. Divers frequently encounter large turtles, eagle rays, groupers, barracuda and sharks. From January through March, humpbacks are often seen in this area.

Interesting swim-throughs cut through the shallow reefs. Snorkelers can see some of the corals and fish life, which reach to within 15ft of the surface, as well as the wreck's remains, though it is deeper and not as easily seen.

The discoverer, Brian Sheedy, found the wreck

Location: 16 miles (26km) S of Salt Cay

Depth Range: 15-40ft (5-12m)

Access: Boat or live-aboard

Expertise Rating: Novice

in 1991 with the help of local historian Josiah Marvel. The best way to see the wreck is to go with Salt Cay Divers, who know the area better than any other operation. The site can be dived year-round, but the best time to dive the wreck is between May and November, when you'll find the calmest conditions and fewest hazards. The currents and surge range from slight to moderate.

CLARK MILLER

Nine anchors lie exposed on the seafloor near the *Endymion* wreck.

Marine Life

The Turks and Caicos Islands have an incredible number and variety of tropical fish and invertebrates—from colorful and unusual reef species to large and magestic pelagics. The marine life depicted below represents species that are commonly seen on the region's protected reefs. The Hazardous Marine Life section focuses on those animals that may present a danger to divers in this region.

Common names are used freely but are notoriously inaccurate and inconsistent. The two-part scientific name, usually shown in italics, is more precise. It consists of a genus name followed by a species name. A genus is a group of closely related species that share common features. A species is a recognizable group within a genus whose members are capable of interbreeding. Where the species or genus is unknown, the naming reverts to the next known level: family (F), order (O), class (C) or phylum (Ph).

Common Vertebrates

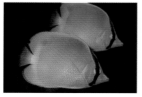

gray angelfish
Pomacanthus arcuatus

queen angelfish
Holacanthus ciliaris

Atlantic spadefish
Chaetodipterus faber

spotfin butterflyfish
Chaetodon ocellatus

spotted drum (juvenile)
Equetus punctatus

indigo hamlet
Hypoplectrus indigo

horse-eye jack
Caranx latus

glasseye snapper
Heteropriacanthus cruentatus

yellow goatfish
Mulloidichthys martinicus

neon goby
Gobiosoma oceanops

squirrelfish
Holocentrus adscensionis

whitespotted filefish
Cantherhines macrocerus

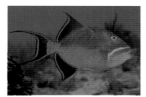

queen triggerfish
Balistes vetula

great barracuda
Sphyraena barracuda

Nassau grouper
Epinephelus striatus

frogfish
Antennarius sp.

Caribbean reef shark
Carcharhinus perezi

nurse shark
Ginglymostoma cirratum

lemon shark
Negaprion brevirostris

humpback whale
Megaptera novaeangliae

bottlenose dolphin
Tursiops truncatus

hawksbill turtle
Eretmochelys imbriocata

green turtle
Chelonia mydas

loggerhead turtle
Caretta caretta

Common Invertebrates

batwing coral crab
Carpilius corallinus

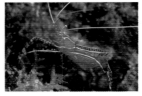

Pederson cleaner shrimp
Periclimenes pedersoni

Caribbean spiny lobster
Panulirus argus

Caribbean reef octopus
Octopus briareus

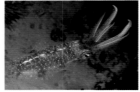

Caribbean reef squid
Sepioteuthis sepioidea

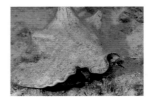

queen conch
Strombus gigas

fingerprint cyphoma
Cyphoma signatum

flamingo tongue
Cyphoma gibbosum

rough fileclam
Lima scabra

Christmas tree worm
Spirobranchus giganteus

social feather duster worm
Bispira brunnea

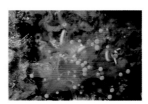

orange ball corallimorpharian
Pseudocorynactis caribbeorum

Hazardous Marine Life

Marine animals almost never attack divers. However, many marine animals possess offensive or defensive weaponry that they will employ if threatened, provoked or annoyed. The ability to recognize hazardous creatures is a valuable asset in avoiding accident and injury. The following are some of the potentially hazardous creatures most commonly found in the Turk and Caicos Islands.

Bristle Worm

Bristle worms, also called fire worms, are found on most reefs. They are free-moving segmented worms that have bundles, or tufts, of sharp detachable hairs around their periphery. These worms average 4 to 6 inches (10 to 15cm) long, but divers have seen 10- to 12-inch (25 to 30cm) specimens feeding on branching corals and gorgonians during night dives at French Cay. The tiny bristles can penetrate the skin, causing a very painful burning sensation. Don't rub the affected area, as this can cause the bristles to spread or penetrate deeper into the skin. A red welt will often appear around the wound. You can remove the embedded bristles with adhesive tape, rubber cement or a commercial facial peel. Apply a decontaminant such as vinegar, rubbing alcohol or dilute ammonia. The irritation usually goes away in a day or two.

Fire Coral

Although often mistaken for stony coral, fire coral is a hydroid colony that secretes a hard, calcareous skeleton. Fire coral grows in many different shapes, often encrusting or taking the form of a variety of reef structures. It is usually identifiable by its tan, mustard or brown color and fingerlike columns with whitish tips. The entire colony is covered by tiny pores and fine, hairlike projections nearly invisible to the unaided eye. Fire coral "stings" by discharging small, specialized cells called nematocysts. Contact causes a burning sensation that lasts for several minutes and may produce red welts on the skin. Do not rub the area, as you will only spread the stinging particles. Cortisone cream can reduce the inflammation, and antihistamine cream is good for killing the pain. Serious stings should be treated by a doctor.

Jellyfish

Jellyfish are translucent, unattached medusae that swim in open water. All have a prominent dome that varies in shape. Trailing from the edge of the dome are nematocyst-bearing tentacles. The number and length of tentacles varies greatly between species. Jellyfish move through the water by the pulsating contractions of the dome. Although only a few jellyfish are toxic, caution should be used with all types of jellyfish. Stings are often irritating but not painful. Some people may have a stronger reaction than others. Thimble jellyfish, which are common in the Turks and Caicos during the spring, affect some people by causing irritating welts, yet have no effect on others. However, stings from box jellyfish can cause severe pain and swelling. Generally, box jellyfish are a problem only on night dives, when they are attracted by the dive boat's bright lights. They will appear in the top 10 or 15ft (3 or 5m) of the water column. Always look up as you ascend. Hit the purge button on your regulator to give the jellyfish a quick burst of air, which will clear them from your path. Stings from any jellyfish should be treated immediately with a decontaminant such as vinegar, rubbing alcohol, baking soda or dilute ammonia.

Scorpionfish

Scorpionfish are well-camouflaged creatures that have poisonous spines along their dorsal fins. They are often difficult to spot since they typically rest quietly on the bottom or on coral, looking more like rocks. Be careful where you put your hands. Scorpionfish wounds can be very painful. To treat a puncture, wash the wound and immerse in hot, nonscalding water for 30 to 90 minutes. You might even try rubbing the area with meat tenderizer to break down the venom. The most common scorpionfish in the Turks and Caicos is the spotted scorpionfish, which can grow to about 10 inches (25cm) long.

Moray Eel

Distinguished by their long, thick, snake-like bodies and tapered heads, eels won't bother you unless you bother them. Moray eels open and close their mouths to force water (and oxygen) over their gills—this is not a sign of aggression. Don't feed them or put your hand in a dark hole—eels have the unfortunate combination of sharp teeth and poor eyesight, and will bite if they feel threatened. If you are bitten, don't try to pull your hand away suddenly—the teeth slant backward and are extraordinarily sharp. Let the

eel release it and then surface slowly. Treat with antiseptics, anti-tetanus and anti-biotics. Morays usually feed at night, using their sense of smell to find prey. Spotted and green moray eels are among the most common in the Turks and Caicos.

Sea Urchin

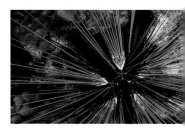

Sea urchins tend to live in shallow areas near shore and come out of their shelters at night. They vary in color and size, with spines ranging from short and blunt to long and needle-sharp. The spines are the urchin's most dangerous weapon, easily able to penetrate neoprene wetsuits, booties and gloves. Treat minor punctures by extracting the spines and immersing the area in nonscalding hot water. More serious injuries require medical attention.

Stingray

Identified by its diamond-shaped body and wide "wings," the stingray has one or two venomous spines at the base of its tail. Stingrays like shallow waters and tend to rest and feed on sand, rubble or eelgrass bottoms, often burying themselves in the sand. Often only the eyes, gill slits and tail are visible. The most common stingray in the Turks and Caicos Islands is the southern stingray. This creature is harmless unless you step on it, sit on it or pull on its tail, which will invoke a defensive response. Though injuries are uncommon, wounds are extremely painful, and often deep and infective. Immerse wound in nonscalding hot water, administer pain medication and seek medical aid.

Sharks

Sharks come in many shapes and sizes. They are most recognizable by their triangular dorsal fin. Though many species are shy, there are occasional attacks. About 25 species worldwide are considered dangerous to humans. Sharks will generally not attack unless provoked, so don't taunt, tease or feed them. Avoid spearfishing, carrying fish baits or mimicking a wounded fish, and your likelihood of being attacked will greatly diminish. Face and quietly watch any shark that is acting aggressively and be prepared to push it away with a camera, knife or tank. If someone is bitten by a shark, stop the bleeding, reassure the patient, treat for shock and seek immediate medical aid.

Diving Conservation & Awareness

The reefs throughout the Turks and Caicos Islands offer lush, healthy corals and sponges, as well as abundant fish populations. Government policy makers and dive operators alike understand that the region's excellent diving environment brings tourists to the country—something both want to see continue.

With this in mind, in 1992 the government established an extensive system of parks designed to protect the scenic environment and wildlife habitats. Thirty-three areas comprising more than 325 sq miles (840sq km) were designated national parks, nature reserves, sanctuaries and sites of historical interest under the jurisdiction of the Department of Environmental and Coastal Resources, Ministry of Natural Resources. The slogan "Beautiful by Nature" was adopted, along with policies to protect wildlife and preserve the islands' natural habitats—both above water and below.

Most local dive businesses operate almost exclusively within the national marine parks. Visitors should expect their dive operator's predive orientation to include information about restrictions and proper diving techniques. Spearfishing, Jet Skiing and diving for lobster and conch are outlawed within the parks.

In 1985 the country's first dive site moorings were placed by Grand Turk dive operators who were concerned about anchor damage to the reefs. Both the government and the National Parks Committee (now the Department of Environmental and Coastal Resources) supported the effort. Dive site preservation is now a national parks' priority. Approximately 40 permanent moorings now protect the Turks and Caicos' reefs. The Ministry of Natural Resources has acquired state-of-the-art equipment to install mooring pins and makes an ongoing effort to add new moorings and replace those that have been torn out. The national parks office keeps up-to-date information on how often each site is visited, as well as the number of divers at each site, based on information provided by the dive operators. For more information, contact the national parks office on Providenciales at ☎ 649-941-5122 or fax 649-946-4793.

The Department of Environmental and Coastal Resources (decr@tciway.tc) has offices on Grand Turk (☎ 649-946-2855; fax 649-946-1895), Providenciales (☎ 649-946-4017; fax 649-941-3063) and South Caicos (☎ 649-946-3306; fax 649-946-3306).

The Turks and Caicos National Trust (P.O. Box 540, Providenciales; ☎ 649-941-4258; fax 649-941-5710; tc.nattrust@tciway.tc) is a nongovernmental organization dedicated to the preservation of the cultural, natural and historical heritage of the islands. The Trust has established three underwater snorkeling trails (two off Provo and another off Grand Turk) and the Little Water Cay Reserve, as well as initiated countrywide studies of bird populations. In 1999 it gained international funding to manage the Ramsar Site wetland sanctuary in North, Middle and East Caicos.

A diver inspects a permanent mooring.

Responsible Diving

Dive sites are often along reefs and walls covered in beautiful corals and sponges. It only takes a moment—an inadvertently placed hand or knee, or a careless brush or kick with a fin—to destroy this fragile, living part of our delicate ecosystem. By following certain basic guidelines while diving, you can help preserve the ecology and beauty of the reefs:

1. Never drop boat anchors onto a coral reef and take care not to ground boats on coral. Encourage dive operators and regulatory bodies in their efforts to establish permanent moorings at appropriate dive sites.

2. Practice and maintain proper buoyancy control and avoid overweighting. Be aware that buoyancy can change over the period of an extended trip. Initially you may breathe harder and need more weighting; a few days later you may breathe more easily and need less weight. Tip: Use your weight belt and tank position to maintain a horizontal position—raise them to elevate your feet, lower

Dive in to Turks and Caicos' National Parks

The Department of Environmental and Coastal Resources has devised different classifications for the protected areas. **National Parks** are areas set aside for responsible recreational use. Each of these parks has special features for visitors to experience. Some national parks encompass both land and sea areas. **Nature Reserves** were established to protect particularly sensitive unique areas or rare species. Development is not allowed in these areas and access is limited. **Sanctuaries** are important breeding or spawning grounds for wildlife. Entry is by permit only. **Historical Sites** are designated to protect and preserve the history and unique heritage of the Turks and Caicos Islands. The following list describes a few of the parks of particular interest to divers.

Providenciales

Northwest Point Marine National Park The beautiful deserted beaches at the northwest end of Provo are accessible only by four-wheel-drive vehicles. Just offshore, within the confines of the park, are a series of excellent dive sites offering majestic stands of elkhorn coral and superb wall diving. Inland saline ponds attract roseate spoonbills and other waterfowl.

Princess Alexandra Marine National Park This park is along the north shore of Provo, between Thompson Cove and Leeward Point, and encompasses Grace Bay. The park affords protection to the onshore and offshore environment along Grace Bay, as well as cays northeast of Provo. Quite a few good dive sites in Grace Bay feature spur-and-groove reefs with walls that drop to a sand bottom in about 95ft (29m). Visitors can enjoy the park's 13 miles (21km) of beautiful sand beaches, as well as a variety of watersports.

Princess Alexandra, Little Water Cay, Mangrove Cay and Donna Cay Nature Reserve This reserve encompasses the north coast of Providenciales from Thompson Cove to the north end of Little Water Cay at the east end of Provo. The reserve provides protection to wildlife, including iguanas, ospreys, pelicans and flamingos, as well as various tropical flora.

Pine Cay

Fort George Land & Sea National Park Just off the north coast of Pine Cay (a small cay northeast of Provo), visitors will discover cannons from the 1790s in only a few feet of water. The cay is home to iguanas and ospreys. Day-boat dive operations from Provo sometimes visit the exceptional sites nearby.

West Caicos

West Caicos Marine National Park This park encompasses the dive sites along the western side of West Caicos, which offers great wall diving offshore and excellent snorkeling close to shore.

Lake Catherine Nature Reserve This scenic park on the west coast of West Caicos protects the breeding grounds of flamingos, ospreys, ducks and waders.

Molasses Reef Wreck Historical Site This wreck site is at Molasses Reef, on the southwest edge of the Caicos Bank between West Caicos and French Cay. This is the earliest known shipwreck site in the western hemisphere (predating 1509). The Turks and Caicos National Museum in Grand Turk displays artifacts from this wreck.

French Cay

French Cay Sanctuary This sanctuary is at the western edge of the Caicos Bank. The small cay is home to nesting seabirds, including frigates, and is also a breeding ground for nurse sharks. In July and August divers can observe large numbers of mating nurse sharks in the sand shallows around the cay. The sharks should not be disturbed during mating. For those interested in observing these creatures, contact Big Blue, which runs excellent ecological tours to the area.

South Caicos

Admiral Cockburn Land & Sea National Park This park is off the south end of South Caicos and east of Long Cay. The area affords protection to the scrub-covered shoreline, as well as the off-shore coral reefs of southern South Caicos.

Grand Turk

Columbus Landfall Marine National Park This park is named for the site that many believe was Christopher Columbus' first landfall in the New World. The park includes Grand Turk's exceptional west wall, most of which is less than 300 yards (275m) offshore and plummets vertically to 7,000ft (2,100m).

Grand Turk Cays Land & Sea National Park This park comprises a series of tiny cays just east of Grand Turk's southeast shore, including Gibb's Cay, Penniston Cay and Martin Alonza Pinzon Cay. It's an important nesting site for seabirds. Turk's head cacti flourish on Martin Alonza Pinzon Cay. A colony of grandly winged frigate birds reside on Penniston. Gibb's Cay has a large population of seabirds, including sooty and noddy terns, that nest there each year in May and June, as well as approachable stingrays in shallow water.

Long Cay Sanctuary Long Cay, southeast of Grand Turk, is a sanctuary for terns, gulls, iguanas and tropical plants.

Salt Cay

Salt Industry Historical Site Visitors will find remnants of the solar salt industry, including salinas and windmills constructed between 1700 and 1960. A number of historical buildings line the waterfront, including the White House (a salt merchant's stately manor home, built in 1835) and an old whaling station.

HMS *Endymion* Historical Site This wreck site south of Salt Cay is where the 140ft (43m) British warship the HMS *Endymion* sank to 40ft (12m) in 1790. Divers will find cannons, anchors, ballast, bronze pins, copper nails and other remains of the wreck.

Visitors to Gibb's Cay can take a close look at southern stingrays.

them to elevate your upper body. Also be careful about buoyancy loss: As you go deeper, your wetsuit compresses, as does the air in your BC.

3. Avoid touching living marine organisms with your body and equipment. Polyps can be damaged by even the gentlest contact. Never stand on or touch living coral. The use of gloves is no longer recommended: Gloves make it too easy to hold on to the reef. The abrasion caused by gloves may be even more damaging to the reef than your hands are. If you must hold on to the reef, touch only exposed rock or dead coral.

4. Take great care in underwater caves. Spend as little time within them as possible, as your air bubbles can damage fragile organisms. Divers should take turns inspecting the interiors of small caves or under ledges to lessen the chances of damaging contact.

5. Be conscious of your fins. Even without contact, the surge from heavy fin strokes near the reef can do damage. Avoid full-leg kicks when diving close to the bottom and when leaving a photo scene. When you inadvertently kick something, stop kicking! It seems obvious, but some divers either panic or are totally oblivious when they bump something. When treading water in shallow reef areas, take care not to kick up clouds of sand. Settling sand can smother the delicate reef organisms.

6. Secure gauges, computer consoles and the octopus regulator so they're not dangling—they are like miniature wrecking balls to a reef.

7. When swimming in strong currents, be extra careful about leg kicks and handholds.

8. Photographers should take extra precautions, as cameras and equipment affect buoyancy. Changing f-stops, framing a subject and maintaining position for a photo often conspire to thwart the ideal "no-touch" approach on a reef. When you must use "holdfasts," choose them intelligently (e.g., use one finger only for leverage off an area of dead coral).

9. Resist the temptation to collect or buy coral or shells. Aside from the ecological damage, collecting marine souvenirs depletes the beauty of a site and spoils other divers' enjoyment.

10. Ensure that you take home all your trash and any litter you may find as well. Plastics in particular pose a serious threat to marine life.

11. Resist the temptation to feed fish. You may disturb their normal eating habits, encourage aggressive behavior or feed them food that is detrimental to their health.

12. Minimize your disturbance of marine animals. Don't ride on the backs of turtles or manta rays, as this can cause them great anxiety.

Listings

Telephone Calls

To call the Turks and Caicos from the U.S., Canada or the Caribbean, dial 1 + 649 + the local seven-digit number. From elsewhere, dial your country's international access code + 649 + the local number. Toll-free (800, 877 or 888) numbers can be accessed from the U.S. and, usually, Canada.

Accommodations

Providenciales

Airport Inn
Airport Plaza, Airport Rd.,
Providenciales
☎ 941-3514 fax: 941-3281
www.provo.net.tcnational
airportinn@provo.net

Allegro Resort & Casino
P.O. Box 205, Grace Bay,
Providenciales
Toll-free ☎ 1-800-858-2258
☎/fax 946-5522
www.allegroresorts.com
allegroresorts@tciway.tc

Beaches Resort & Spa
P.O. Box 186, Grace Bay,
Providenciales
Toll-free ☎ 1-800-232-2437
☎ 946-8000 fax: 946-8001
www.beaches.com

Beach Trees (Villa)
Providenciales
☎ 946-5820

Calypso House (Villa)
Ocean Point, Providenciales
Toll-free ☎ 1-800-643-2554
fax: 415-897-8095
www.tcivillas.com

**Carriage House at
   Turtle Watch** (Villa)
Turtle Cove Canal,
Providenciales
☎ 941-5458 fax: 941-5510
unicorn@tciway.tc

Carribean Paradise Inn
P.O. Box 673, Grace Bay,
Providenciales
☎ 946-5020 or 941-6758
fax: 946-5022
www.paradise.tc
inn@paradise.tc

Casuarina Cottages (Villa)
c/o Caribbean Place
P.O. Box 279, Providenciales
☎ 946-4474 fax: 946-4433
www.tcrealty.com
tcrealty@tciway.tc

Citadel Seascape Villas (Villa)
Turtle Cove, Providenciales
☎/fax: 941-4196
www.citadelvillas.com
citadelvillas@tciway.tc

Club Med Turkoise
Grace Bay Rd., Providenciales
☎ 946-5491 to 5496
fax: 946-5497
www.clubmed.com

Coconut Grove (Villa)
P.O. Box 257, Leeward Hwy,
Providenciales
☎ 946-5431 fax: 941-4533
saunders@tciway.tc

Comfort Suites
P.O. Box 315, Providenciales
Toll-free ☎ 1-888-678-3483
☎ 946-8888 fax: 946-5444
comfort@provo.net
www.provo.net/comfort

**Coral Gardens &
   White House Villa**
Grace Bay, Providenciales
Toll-free ☎ 1-800-532-8536
☎ 941-3713 fax: 941-5171
www.coralgardens.com
coralgardens@tciway.tc

Crystal Bay Condominiums
Northwest Point, Providenciales
☎ 941-5555 fax: 941-5839
www.crystalbay.tc
crystalbay@tciway.tc

Doc's Cove Beach House (Villa)
Turtle Cove, Providenciales
☎ 946-4256 fax: 941-3406
bonefish@tciway.tc

**Elliot Holdings & Manta
   Management Co.** (Villa)
P.O. Box 235, Providenciales
☎ 946-5355 fax: 946-5176
www.provo.net/elliot/
elliot@provo.net

Erebus Inn
P.O. Box 238, Turtle Cove,
Providenciales
Toll-free ☎ 1-800-323-5655
☎ 946-4240 fax: 946-4704
www.erebus.tc
erebus@tciway.tc

Grace Bay Club
P.O. Box 128, Grace Bay,
Providenciales
Toll-free ☎ 1-800-946-5757
☎ 946-5050 fax: 946-5758
www.gracebayclub.com

Providenciales (continued)

Harbour Club Villas (Villa)
Venetian Way, Providenciales
☎/fax: 941-5748
www.harbourclub.org
info@harbourclub.org

Le Deck Hotel & Bay Bistro
(Also carries name **Sibonne**)
P.O. Box 144, Providenciales,
Toll-free ☎ 1-800-223-9815
☎ 946-5547 fax: 946-5770
www.provo.net/ledeck
ledeck@tciway.tc

Market Place Villas (Villa)
P.O. Box 170, Market Place,
Providenciales
☎ 946-4919 or 941-0676
fax: 941-5880
www.marketplacevillas.com
info@marketplacevillas.com

Ocean Club Condominiums
P.O. Box 240, Grace Bay,
Providenciales
Toll-free ☎ 1-800-457-8787
☎ 946-5880 fax: 946-5845
www.ocean-club.com
oceanclb@tciway.tc

Ocean Point Villas (Villa)
Sapodilla Bay, Providenciales
☎ 404-351-2200 (U.S.)
fax: 404-351-2615 (U.S.)

Platinum Resort Villas (Villa)
Providenciales

☎ 946-5539 fax: 946-5421
prvillas@tciway.tc

Point Grace
P.O. Box 700, Grace Bay,
Providenciales
☎ 946-5548 fax: 946-5543
www.pointgrace.tc
pointgrace@tciway.tc

Prestigious Properties (Villa)
P.O. Box 23, Prestige Place,
Providenciales
☎ 946-4379 fax: 946-4703
www.prestigiousproperties.com
sales@prestigiousproperties.com

The Sands
P.O. Box 681, Grace Bay,
Providenciales
Toll-free ☎ 1-800-456-6686
☎ 946-5199 fax: 946-5198
www.thesandsresort.com
thesands@tciway.tc

The Seagate (Villa)
P.O. Box 505, Penn's Rd.,
Providenciales
☎/fax: 946-4706
www.provo.net/seagate
seagate@provo.net

Serendipity (Villa)
P.O. Box 483, Providenciales
☎/fax: 946-4787
www.provo.net/dipity
dipity@provo.net

**South Fleetwood Apartment
& Cottages** (Villa)
Grace Bay, Providenciales
☎ 946-5376 fax: 946-5792

TC Safari (Villa)
P.O. Box 64, The Market Place,
Providenciales
☎ 941-5043 fax: 946-4939
tcsafari@tc

Treasure Beach Villas (Villa)
Grace Bay, Providenciales
☎ 946-4325 fax: 946-4934
provo.net/treasurebeach/
treasurebeach@tciway.tc

Turtle Cove Inn
P. O. Box 131, Turtle Cove,
Providenciales
Toll-free ☎ 1-800-887-0477
☎ 946-4203 fax: 946-4141
www.turtlecoveinn.com
turtlecoveinn@provo.net

Villa Camilla (Villa)
Grace Bay, Providenciales
☎ 617-731-2194
www.villa-camilla.com

Villa Oasis (Villa)
Providenciales
☎ 941-5556 fax: 941-3344
www.villaoasis.com

Parrot Cay

Parrot Cay (Villa)
Parrot Cay
☎ 946-7788 fax: 946-7789
www.parrot-cay.com
parrot@tciway.tc

Pine Cay

The Meridian Club (Villa)
Pine Cay
Toll-free ☎ 1-800-331-9154
☎ 203-602-0300 (U.S.) fax: 203-602-2265 (U.S.)
www.meridianclub.com

Grand Turk

Arawak Inn & Beach Club
P.O. Box 190, Governor's
Beach, Grand Turk
☎ 946-2276 or 946-2277
fax: 946-2279
www.arawakinn.com
reservations@arawakinn.com

Arches of Grand Turk (Villa)
P.O. Box 226, North Ridge,
Grand Turk
☎/fax: 946-2941
www.grandturkarches.com
archesgrandturk@tciway.tc

**Coral Reef Beach
Resort & Villas**
P.O. Box 190, Windward Shore,
Grand Turk

Toll-free ☎ 1-800-418-4704
☎ 946-2055 fax: 946-2911
gthotels@tciway.tc

Island House
P.O. Box 36, Lighthouse Rd.,
Grand Turk
☎ 946-1388 fax: 946-2646
www.islandhouse-tci.com
ishouse@tciway.tc

Grand Turk (continued)

Osprey Beach Hotel
P.O. Box 1, Duke St.,
Grand Turk
☎ 946-2260 fax: 946-2817
www.ospreybeachhotel.com
info@ospreybeachhotel.com

Sadler's Seaview Apartments
(Villa)
Duke St., Grand Turk

☎ 946-2569 or 946-2374
fax: 946-1523

Salt Raker Inn
P.O. Box 1, Duke St.,
Grand Turk
☎ 946-2260 fax: 946-2646
sraker@tciway.tc

Turks Head Hotel
P.O. Box 58, Duke St.,
Grand Turk

☎ 946-2466 fax: 946-1716
www.grand-turk.com
tophotel@grand-turk.com

The Waters Edge Club (Villa)
Grand Turk
Toll-free ☎ 1-800-577-3872
☎ 946-2055 fax: 946-2911
gthotels@tciway.tc

Salt Cay

Castaways Beach House
Salt Cay
☎ 946-6921 fax: 946-6922
☎ 1-315-536-7061 (U.S.)
fax: 1-315-536-0737 (U.S.)
viking@vivanet.com

Halfway Guest House
Salt Cay
☎ 946-6936

Mount Pleasant Guest House
Salt Cay
☎/fax: 946-6927
www.mountpleasantsaltcay.com
mtpleasantinfo@yahoo.com

Pirates Hideaway
Victoria St., Salt Cay
☎/fax: 946-6909
www.windnet.com/pirate

Salt Cay Sunset House
Victoria St., Salt Cay
☎/fax: 946-6942
www.seaone.org
seaone@tciway.tc

Sunset Reef
Salt Cay
Toll-free ☎ 888-858-3483
☎ 410-889-3662
fax: 410-467-5744

www.sunsetreef.com
info@sunsetreef.com

Tradewinds Guest Suites
Victoria St., Salt Cay
☎ 946-6906 fax: 946-6940
www.tradewinds.tc
tradewinds@tciway.tc

Windmills Plantation Hotel
Salt Cay
Toll-free ☎ 1-800-822-7715
☎ 946-6962 fax: 946-6930
www.windmillsplantation.com
plantation@saltcaysite.com

South Caicos

Mae's Bed & Breakfast
South Caicos
☎ 946-3207

South Caicos Ocean Haven
West St., South Caicos
☎ 946-3444 fax: 946-3446

www.oceanhaven.tc
divesouth@tciway.tc

Diving Services

The Turks and Caicos Islands have several excellent dive operations and snorkeling tour services. Given the anticipated increase in tourism, the number of diving and snorkeling services is likely to grow significantly over the next few years.

You can expect dive shops here to provide well-maintained and safe equipment, air fills and facilities. Most dive stores offer quality rental gear, though the selection may be limited, especially on the smaller islands. Excellent certification programs (most often PADI or NAUI) and friendly, professional personnel are standard at most shops. All operators offer Open Water referral courses, so you can complete the book and pool work at home and do the checkout dives in TCI.

While most dive shops are owned and operated independent of the island hotels, you may be able to book a dive package that includes both diving and lodging at a reputable hotel or resort. Generally, the dive operations provide transfers, or pick-up and drop-off, from the hotels.

Providenciales

Beluga Charters
P.O. Box 385, Providenciales
☎/fax: 946-4396
sailbeluga@tciway.tc
Dive Shop: no **Rentals:** no
Air: no **Courses:** no
Boat: *Beluga* (37ft catamaran)
Trips: Private day-sailing charters with snorkeling

Big Blue Unlimited
Leeward Marina,
P.O. Box 159, Providenciales
☎ 946-5034 or 941-6455
fax: 946-5033
www.bigblue.tc
bigblue@tciway.tc
Dive Shop: yes **Rentals:** yes
Air: yes **Courses:** yes
Boats: *Live and Direct* (40ft power catamaran, 8 divers), *Yes - I* (27ft power catamaran, 6 divers)
Trips: Provo, West Caicos, French Cay
Other: Nitrox/tri-mix; kayak and bike rentals and tours; hiking tours

Caicos Adventures
Caicos Café Plaza,
P.O. Box 47, Providenciales
☎/fax: 941-3346
www.caicosadventures.tc
divucrzy@tciway.tc
Dive Shop: yes **Rentals:** yes
Air: yes **Courses:** yes (PADI/NAUI/Universal)
Boats: *Melissa II* (40ft, 14 divers), *Caicos Cat Express* (43ft, 16 divers)
Trips: West Caicos, French Cay, Molasses Reef, Sandbore Channel, Southwest Reef, West Sand Spit
Other: Lunch and drink on every trip, hotel/dive packages, hotel transfers

Dive Provo
Ports of Call and Allegro Resort & Casino,
P.O. Box 413, Providenciales
Toll-free ☎ 1-800-234-7768
☎ 946-5029 fax: 946-5936
www.diveprovo.com
diving@diveprovo.com
Dive Shop: yes **Rentals:** yes
Air: yes **Courses:** yes (PADI)

Boats: *Explorer* (42ft, 16 divers), *Conquest* (36ft, 18 divers), *Star* (42ft, 20 divers)
Trips: Grace Bay, Pine Cay, Northwest Point, West Caicos and French Cay

Flamingo Divers
Turtle Cove Landing,
P.O. Box 322, Providenciales
Toll-free ☎ 1-800-204-9282
☎/fax: 946-4193
www.provo.net/flamingo
flamingo@provo.net
Dive Shop: yes **Rentals:** yes
Air: yes **Courses:** yes
Boats: *British Spirit* (28ft, 10 divers), *Adios* (28ft, 10 divers)
Trips: Northwest Point, West Caicos, French Cay

J & B Tours
Leeward Marina,
P.O. Box 416, Providenciales
☎ 946-5047 fax: 946-5288
www.jbtours.com
jill@jbtours.com
Dive Shop: no **Rentals:** yes
Air: no **Courses:** no
Boats: *Cool Runnins* (6 divers), *Seabreeze* (6 divers)
Trips: Snorkeling trips around Providenciales and French Cay, private boat charters

02 Technical Diving
P.O. Box 150, Providenciales
☎/fax: 941-3499
www.o2technicaldiving.com
john@o2technicaldiving.com
Dive Shop: no **Rentals:** yes
Air: yes (nitrox and tri-mix available) **Courses:** yes (IANTD/TDI/BSAC/PADI)
Boats: Chartered
Trips: Rebreather and Advanced Extended Range dives to unexplored sites

Ocean Outback Adventures
P.O. Box 323, Providenciales
☎ 941-5810
www.provo.net/oceanoutback
oceanoutback@provo.net
Dive Shop: no **Rentals:** no
Air: yes **Courses:** no
Boat: *Island Diver* (65ft, 16 divers)
Trips: Providenciales and surrounding cays

Ocean Vibes Scuba & Watersports
P.O. Box 584, Turtle Cove Marina, Providenciales
Toll-free ☎ 1-877-426-7626
☎ 231-6636 fax: 941-3141
www.oceanvibes.com
oceanvibes@tciway.tc
Dive Shop: yes **Rentals:** yes
Air: yes **Courses:** yes (NAUI/PADI)
Boats: Sport Craft (28ft, 6 divers), Sun Tracker (24ft, 10 snorkelers)
Trips: Pine Cay, Grace Bay and Northwest Point; day trips to barrier reef, Little Water Cay, uninhabited cays and reserves
Other: Underwater scooter rentals and tours available

Provo Turtle Divers
Turtle Cove Marina,
P.O. Box 219, Providenciales (satellite shops at Ocean Club and Ocean Club West)
Toll-free ☎ 800-833-1341
☎ 946-4232 fax: 941-5296
www.provoturtledivers.com
provoturtledivers@provo.net
Dive Shop: yes **Rentals:** yes
Air: yes **Courses:** yes (PADI NAUI/ Universal Referrals)
Boats: *Chuck's Honey* (42ft, 22 divers), *Chuck's Other Honey* (30ft, 12 divers)
Trips: Providenciales (Grace Bay, Pine Cay, Northwest Point, West Caicos and French Cay); private charters

Silver Deep
Leeward Marina,
P.O. Box 644, Providenciales
☎ 946-5612 fax: 946-4527
www.silverdeep.com
silverdeep_dean@tciway.tc
Dive Shop: yes **Rentals:** yes
Air: yes **Courses:** no
Boats: Four boats (21-27ft, 8-16 divers)
Trips: Private charters to Pine Cay, Grace Bay, Northwest Point, West Caicos & French Cay
Other: Half-day and full-day cruises to Little Water Cay, West Caicos, North Caicos and Middle Caicos for snorkeling, beachcombing and BBQ

South Caicos

South Caicos Ocean Haven
West St., South Caicos
☎ 946-3444 fax: 946-3446
www.oceanhaven.tc
divesouth@tciway.tc

Dive Shop: yes **Rentals:** yes
Air: yes **Courses:** yes
Boats: Two 24ft Carolina skiffs
(maximum 10 divers per boat)

Trips: Local morning, afternoon and night dives
Other: Accommodations and
dining available on site

Grand Turk

Blue Water Divers
P.O. Box 124, Grand Turk
☎/fax: 946-2432
www.grandturkscuba.com
info@grandturkscuba.com,
mrolling@tciway.tc
Dive Shop: yes **Rentals:** yes
Air: yes (nitrox available)
Courses: yes (PADI)
Boats: *Dancing Fool* (24ft, 10
divers), *Calypso Cruiser* (24ft,
8 divers)
Trips: South Caicos, Salt Cay,
Gibb's Cay and *Endymion*
wreck
Other: Snorkeling trips

Sea Eye Diving
P.O. Box 67, Grand Turk
Toll-free ☎ 1-800-513-5823
☎/fax: 946-1407
www.seaeyediving.com
ci@tciway.tc
Dive Shop: yes **Rentals:** yes
Air: yes (nitrox available)
Courses: yes (PADI/NAUI)
Boats: Six 24ft boats carry 8
divers each; one 45ft boat for
large groups
Trips: South Caicos, Grand
Turk, Gibb's Cay and Salt Cay
Other: On-staff underwater
photographers, camera lab, E6
processing, nitrox instruction

Oasis Divers
P.O. Box 137, Grand Turk
Toll-free ☎ 1-800-892-3995
☎/fax: 946-1128
www.oasisdivers.com
oasisdiv@tciway.tc
Dive Shop: yes **Rentals:** yes
Air: yes (nitrox available)
Courses: yes
Boats: Four 24ft Carolina skiffs;
one 30ft Concept boat; small
groups on each boat
Trips: South Caicos, Grand
Turk, Gibb's Cay and Salt Cay
Other: Whale watching and
snorkeling excursions

Salt Cay

Salt Cay Divers
Salt Cay
☎ 946-6906 fax: 946-6922
www.saltcaydivers.tc
scdivers@tciway.tc
Dive Shop: yes **Rentals:** yes
Air: yes **Courses:** yes
Boats: Carolina skiffs (24ft, 8
divers)

Trips: Grand Turk, Gibb's Cay,
Salt Cay, HMS *Endymion*
Other: Snorkeling trips,
specialize in junior and family
certification

Reef Runners
Salt Cay
☎ 946-6927 fax: 946-6960

or ☎ 912-233-1059 (U.S.)
www.reefrunners.com
reefrunners@go.com
Dive Shop: no **Rentals:** no
Air: no **Courses:** no
Trips: Grand Turk, Salt Cay,
HMS *Endymion* and
Gibb's Cay

Live-Aboards

Aggressor Fleet
P.O. Box 1470
Morgan City, LA 70381-1470
Toll-free ☎ 1-800-348-2628
fax: 985-348-0817 (U.S.)
www.aggressor.com
info@aggressor.com
Turks & Caicos Aggressor
Home Port: Providenciales and
Grand Turk
Description: 100ft aluminum
monohull
Accommodations: 5 double
cabins, 1 quad; each has
private bath, TV/VCR and hair
dryer

Destinations: March-January
from Providenciales to West
Caicos, French Cay and West
Sand Spit.
February-April humpback whale
trips from Grand Turk to Silver
Banks.
Season: Year-round
Passengers: 14
Other: Air-conditioning, E6
processing, photo pro on-board,
Open Water referrals, battery
charging tables, hot tub, email
access, nitrox, rebreathers,
kayaks, U/W scooters.

Peter Hughes Diving
5723 NW 159th St.
Miami Lakes, FL 33014 USA
Toll-free ☎ 1-800-932-6237
www.peterhughes.com
dancer@peterhughes.com
Sea Dancer
Home Port: Providenciales
Description: 110ft aluminum
monohull
Accommodations: 9 staterooms
Destinations: Northwest Point,
West Caicos and French Cay
Season: Year-round
Passengers: 18
Other: Air-conditioning, E6
processing, photo pro on-board.

Live-Aboards (continued)

Peter Hughes Diving
(continued)

Wind Dancer
Home Port: Grand Turk
Description: 120ft steel mono-hull
Accommodations: 10 state-rooms
Destinations: April-January: South Caicos, Grand Turk, Salt Cay; January-March: Whale-watching trips to the Silver Banks
Season: Year-round
Passengers: 20
Other: Air-conditioning, camera and video rental and

instruction, E6 processing, photo pro on-board, battery charging tables.

Tao Liveaboard Charters
PMB #461,
88005 Overseas Hwy #9
Islanmorada, FL 33036-3087
Toll-free ☎ 1-800-326-4831
☎ 519-855-6115 (U.S.)
fax: 519-855-6069 (U.S.)
www.sailtao.com
info@sailtao.com

Tao
Home Port: Providenciales
Description: 56ft trimaran

Accommodations: 4 cabins, single berths on request
Destinations: throughout the Turks and Caicos; southern Bahamas
Season: Year-round
Passengers: 8
Other: Custom multi-activity itineraries for small groups and families; diving, snorkeling, sailing, beachcombing. Wind-surfing rig, camera rental, E6 processing, battery charging tables.

Photography & Videography

Finest Foto
Providenciales
☎ 946-5171

Fish Frames Underwater Photography
Neptune Plaza, P.O. Box 96, Providenciales
☎ 946-5841
fishframes@tciway.tc
www.fishframes.com

Island Photo
Tower Plaza, Providenciales
☎ 946-4686

Pennylaine Photo Studio
Central Square, Leeward Highway, Providenciales
☎ 941-3549 fax: 946-5351

Tropical Imaging
Unit 5, Neptune Plaza, Providenciales
☎/fax 946-4059
www.tropicalimaging.com

Village 1-Hour Photo
Leeward Highway, Providenciales
☎ 941-4559

Tourist Offices

The Turks and Caicos Islands Tourist Board has its headquarters (☎ 946-2321, 800-241-0824, fax 946-2733, www.turksandcaicostourism.com, tci.tourism@tciway.tc) on Front Street in Cockburn Town, Grand Turk; its mailing address is P.O. Box 128, Cockburn Town, Grand Turk, Turks and Caicos, BWI. The board is under the jurisdiction of the Ministry of Tourism (☎ 649-946-2801, fax 649-946-1120).

The board also has two information bureaus on Providenciales: at Providenciales Airport (☎ 941-5496) and at Turtle Cove Marina Plaza (☎ 946-4970, fax 941-5494).

The board maintains offices abroad at the following locales:

Turks & Caicos Information Office
c/o MKI, Mitre House
66 Abbey Rd., Enfield,
Middx EN1 2RQ
☎ 020-8350-1017
fax: 020-8350-1011
tricia@ttg.co.uk

Turks & Caicos Islands Tourist Board
11645 Biscayne Blvd, Suite 302
Miami, FL 33181
Toll-free ☎ 1-800-241-0824

Index

dive sites covered in this book appear in **bold** type

Lonely Planet Pisces Books

The **Diving & Snorkeling** guides cover top destinations worldwide. Beautifully illustrated with full-color photos throughout, the series explores the best diving and snorkeling areas and prepares divers for what to expect when they get there. Each site is described in detail, with information on suggested ability levels, depth, visibility and, of course, marine life. There's basic topside information as well for each destination.

Also check out dive guides to:

Australia's Great Barrier Reef	Chuuk Lagoon, Pohnpei & Kosrae	Pacific Northwest	Seychelles
Australia: Southeast Coast	Cocos Island	Palau	Southern California & the Channel Islands
Bali & Lombok	Curaçao	Papua New Guinea	Tahiti & French Polynesia
Baja California	Guam & Yap	Red Sea	Texas
Bermuda	Jamaica	Roatan & Honduras' Bay Islands	Thailand
Bonaire	Monterey Peninsula & Northern California	Scotland	Vanuatu